# The History and Implications of the Dead Sea Scrolls:

*What They Tell Us About Scripture and Questions They Have Raised*

Perry L. Denker, Ph.D.

The History and Implications of the Dead Sea Scrolls
Author: Perry L Denker

All rights reserved
Copyright © 2024 by Perry Denker

No part of this publication may be reproduced, distributed or transmitted in any form or by any means, including photocopying, recording, or other electronic or mechanical methods, without the prior written permission of the publisher, except in the case of brief quotations embodied in critical reviews and certain other noncommercial uses permitted by copyright law.

Published by Perry Denker
ISBN: 978-0255658539

First Edition

*This book is dedicated to my daughter, Courtney, who, many years ago, showed me the way through her example of living as a humble and dedicated follower of Christ.*

*I also want to express my gratitude to Brigid, who was extremely helpful in editing the initial manuscript.*

# About the Author

Perry L. Denker, Ph.D., an impassioned scholar on a quest to deepen our understanding of the Bible, holds a doctoral degree in Biblical Studies from Newburgh Theological Seminary and an MBA from St. Ambrose University. Perry's recent academic journey has been dedicated to unraveling the intricacies of history and scripture, resulting in his inaugural literary work. His debut book, "The History and Implications of the Dead Sea Scrolls," delves into the profound mysteries of these ancient texts, offering insights into their historical significance and the complex questions they pose about scripture. Join Perry on a contemplative journey into their discovery and the wisdom nestled within these ancient manuscripts.

# Table of Contents

| | |
|---|---|
| Table of Contents | v |
| List of Pictures and Tables | x |
| Foreword | xii |

### INTRODUCTION    1
    The Scrolls Discovery    2
    The Scrolls Acquisition    4

### PART ONE: SOCIETY, SETTLEMENT, SITE, AND SCROLLS

### CHAPTER 1: SOCIETY    7
    1.1 Ancient World of the Scrolls    7
    1.2 Historical Events and Period Rule    8
    1.3 Near East Jewish Religious Sects    16

### CHAPTER 2: SETTLEMENT    19
    2.1 Theories of the Qumran Sect    19
    2.2 Khirbet Qumran    20
    2.3 Artifacts    24

### CHAPTER 3: SITE    30
    3.1 The Dead Sea Scroll Caves    30
    3.2 More Sites in the Judean Desert    35

## CHAPTER 4: SCROLLS CREATION AND EVALUATION     **38**

    4.1 Languages and Scripts     38
    4.2 Scribes     40
    4.3 Dating the Scrolls     41
    4.4 Reconstructing     45
    4.5 Cataloging the Scrolls     46

## PART TWO: UNDERSTANDING AND UNVEILING THE SCROLLS

## CHAPTER 5: EDITORIAL PROCESS AND PUBLICATION     **49**

    5.1 Scrolls Editorial Team     49
    5.2 Challenges and Delays     50
    5.3 Team Leadership     52
    5.4 Criticism and Controversy     53
    5.5 Team Evolution and Expansion     55
    5.6 Freeing the Scrolls     55
    5.7 Publication of the Scrolls     56
    5.8 Institutions Central to the Scrolls     57
    5.9 Figures in the Scrolls' Journey     62

## CHAPTER 6: ANCIENT SOURCES     **67**

    6.1 Ancient Religious Texts: The Big Three     67
    6.2 Additional Ancient Manuscripts     69
    6.3 Ancient Historians and Writings     74

## PART THREE: SCROLLS REVEALED

## CHAPTER 7: THE SCROLLS UNCOVERED    78
    7.1 An Overview    78
    7.2 Scroll Fragments Note    79
    7.3 The First Seven Scrolls    80

## CHAPTER 8: RELIGIOUS MANUSCRIPTS    85
    8.1 Biblical Manuscripts    85
        8.1.1 Genesis – Deuteronomy    88
        8.1.2 Samuel    88
        8.1.3 Ezra / Nehemiah    89
        8.1.4 Esther    90
        8.1.5 Psalms    91
        8.1.6 Isaiah    92
        8.1.7 Daniel    93
    8.2 Apocrypha, Pseudepigrapha, and Deuterocanonical Books    95
        8.2.1 1 Enoch    97
        8.2.2 Epistle of Jeremiah    98
        8.2.3 Jubilees    98
        8.2.4 Maccabees    99
        8.2.5 Psalms 151-155    100
        8.2.6 Testament of Levi    101
        8.2.7 Tobit    102
        8.2.8 Wisdom of Sirach (Ben Sirah)    102

## CHAPTER 9: NON-BIBLICAL RELIGIOUS MANUSCRIPTS — 104

- 9.1 Genesis Apocryphon — 104
- 9.2 Thanksgiving Hymns or Hodayot — 105
- 9.3 Pesher on Habakkuk — 106
- 9.4 Temple Scroll — 106
- 9.5 Reworked Pentateuch — 107
- 9.6 Additional Extracanonical Texts — 109

## CHAPTER 10: SECULAR AND COMMUNITY MANUSCRIPTS — 111

- 10.1 Halakhic Letter / 4QMMT — 111
- 10.2 Community Rule (Manual of Discipline) — 112
- 10.3 Copper Scroll — 113
- 10.4 Damascus Document — 115
- 10.5 War Scroll — 116

# PART FOUR: ISSUES, IMPLICATIONS, AND INSIGHTS

## CHAPTER 11: ISSUES AND THEMES IN THE SCROLLS — 119

- 11.1 Apocalypse, Eschatological, End of Days — 119
- 11.2 Calendar: Lunar and Solar — 121
- 11.3 Communal Property and Initiation — 122
- 11.4 Dualism: Light and Darkness — 124
- 11.5 Festivals — 125
- 11.6 Figures (Characters) in the Scrolls — 126
- 11.7 Law, Legal, and Punishment — 128
- 11.8 Marriage and Celibacy — 129

| | |
|---|---|
| 11.9 Messiah / Two Messiahs | 131 |
| 11.10 Purity | 132 |
| 11.11 "The Way" | 133 |

## CHAPTER 12: IMPLICATIONS AND INSIGHTS FROM THE SCROLLS — 135

| | |
|---|---|
| 12.1 Authoritative Books | 135 |
|     12.1.1 Determining Relative Importance | 136 |
|     12.1.2 Texts Possibly Considered Scriptural by the Qumranites | 137 |
| 12.2 Canon | 139 |
| 12.3 Hebrew Bible / Old Testament | 140 |
|     12.3.1 Differences | 141 |
|     12.3.2 Similarities | 141 |
| 12.4 Jesus of Nazareth | 142 |
| 12.5 New Testament | 143 |

## CONCLUSION — 144

| | |
|---|---|
| The Takeaways | 144 |
| The Big Takeaway: Link to Early Christianity | 147 |
| The Legacy of the Dead Sea Scrolls | 149 |
| Concluding Thought | 150 |

| | |
|---|---|
| Appendix A. Glossary | 152 |
| Appendix B. Figures in the Scrolls' Journey | 160 |
| Appendix C. Notes | 167 |
| Appendix D. Bibliography | 177 |

## List of Pictures and Tables

### Pictures                                        Page

| | | |
|---|---|---|
| 1 | Scroll Fragment | xiv |
| 2 | Wall Street Journal Advertisement | 5 |
| 3 | Qumran Region Aerial Image | 21 |
| 4 | Qumran Region Map | 21 |
| 5 | Khirbet Qumran Aerial View | 24 |
| 6 | Scroll Jars and Coins | 26 |
| 7 | Qumran Caves Aerial Views | 31 |
| 8 | Cave 4 Interior | 32 |
| 9 | Scrollery - Scroll Room | 47 |
| 10 | Shrine of the Book Exterior | 60 |
| 11 | Shrine of the Book Interior Displays | 61 |
| 12 | Scroll Figures - Bedouin Men | 64 |
| 13 | Scroll Figures - Metropolitan Samuel | 64 |
| 14 | Scroll Figures - Eleazar Sukenik | 65 |
| 15 | Scroll Figures - Yaegel Yadin | 65 |
| 16 | Scroll Figures - John Trever | 66 |
| 17 | Scroll Figures - Roland de Vaux | 66 |
| 18 | Great Isaiah Scroll | 82 |
| 19 | Great Isaiah Scroll (2) | 93 |
| 20 | Copper Scroll | 114 |

| Tables | | Page |
|---|---|---|
| 1 | Ancient Political and Military Events | 15 |
| 2 | Qumran Occupancy Periods | 22 |
| 3 | Site Fragments Found | 34 |
| 4 | Language of the Scrolls | 39 |
| 5 | Ancient Literary Milestones | 73 |
| 6 | First Seven Scrolls Discovered | 84 |
| 7 | Bible Books Found at Qumran | 87 |

# Foreword

What an incredible journey to explore the very times of our Lord from documents written before, during, and after Jesus' reign on earth as God and man. The Dead Sea Scrolls are concrete representations of at least one segment that existed at the time in what is largely believed to be a precursor to modern Christianity. They are shrouded in questions, never-reconcilable speculation, and even questionable conclusions. Yet, they preserve and illuminate a time in Judeo-Christian heritage that remarkably documents, and in some cases forecasts, what we now know as modern Christianity.

In this book, we explore how the Dead Sea Scrolls have affirmed Christian doctrine, influenced thinking on ancient religious manuscripts, raised questions about certain non-canonical books, and provided insight into the Judeo-Christian beliefs and cultures of the time. What do they tell us about the Bible, and what do they leave unexplained? How has their discovery influenced Christian biblical understanding?

We inspect the scrolls' history, the travails of their discovery and liberation, and the figures that brought them to life in our time and within the texts of old. We also look at the scrolls themselves and focus on the illumination they provide to sacred Judeo-Christian doctrine and, particularly, the Bible.

The discovery of the Dead Sea Scrolls is one of the greatest archaeological, historical, and religious finds of the 20th century. The scrolls provide insights into the history and beliefs of their time, and importantly, they underscore and accentuate a precursor to early Christianity.

Thank you for joining in this journey!

– Perry Denker

# Picture 1

***Isaiah Scroll Fragment.*** A portion of the second discovered copy of the Isaiah Scroll (Isa 57:17 - 59:9), 1QIsa[b]
Public Domain. https://en.wikipedia.org/wiki/Dead_Sea_Scrolls #/media/File:1QIsa_b.jpg

# Introduction

The Dead Sea Scrolls comprise a collection of Jewish documents found between 1947 and 1956 near the Dead Sea in the Judean desert. These texts include fragments from almost every book of the Hebrew Bible (also known as the Old Testament) and other Jewish texts such as hymns, prayers, and philosophical writings. The texts are primarily written in Hebrew, Aramaic, and Greek and provide valuable insights into the beliefs and practices of the Jewish people in the Second Temple period, 516 Before Common Era (BCE) to 70 Common Era (CE).

The discovery of the Dead Sea Scrolls has been of great significance to the study of the Bible, particularly the Hebrew Bible. One of the most important aspects of the scrolls is that they provide scholars with access to much older versions of biblical texts than previously available. The scrolls date from 250 BCE to 68 CE. Prior to the unearthing of the Dead Sea Scrolls, the most ancient existing manuscripts of the Hebrew Bible originated in the 9th to 10th century CE.

The Dead Sea Scrolls have helped scholars better understand the development and transmission of biblical texts over time. They have also offered significant insights into the beliefs and rituals of the Jewish society responsible for creating and safeguarding these writings.

Additionally, the scrolls shed light on the cultural and historical context in which the Hebrew Bible was written and have contributed to the ongoing study of the text and its interpretation.

The Scrolls also raise important questions and debates within biblical studies. For example, some scholars have argued that the scrolls provide evidence of alternative Jewish beliefs and practices that were suppressed by the mainstream Jewish community. Others have argued that the scrolls offer proof of a more diverse and complex Judaism than previously thought. Still, others have argued that the scrolls provide evidence of a more fluid and dynamic process of textual transmission than previously believed.

The Dead Sea Scrolls are a valuable source of information about the Hebrew Bible and the beliefs and practices of the Jewish people in the Second Temple period. They provide important insights into the history and development of the text of the Hebrew Bible and shed light on the broader cultural and social context in which these texts were produced. At the same time, they raise important questions and debates that continue to be explored by scholars today.

***The Scrolls Discovery***

The discovery of the Dead Sea Scrolls is a fascinating story that involves a group of Bedouin shepherd boys, an antiquities dealer, and several Israeli and American scholars.

The Dead Sea Scrolls were found in a series of discoveries between 1947 and 1956 in the vicinity of the Dead Sea. The first scrolls were discovered in 1947 by three Bedouin shepherds named Muhammed edh-Dhib and his cousins Jum'a Muhammed and Khalil Musa, who stumbled upon a cave near the ancient site of Qumran while looking for a lost sheep. The story goes that one of the boys threw a rock into the cave, attempting to get the sheep to vacate the cave. Instead, they heard the sound of a clay jar breaking. Inside the cave, they found several clay jars containing scrolls made of parchment.

Many months later, the shepherds took the scrolls to a local antiquities dealer, who recognized their potential value and contacted scholars at the Hebrew University in Jerusalem. Several scholars were involved in the initial study of the scrolls, and they determined that the scrolls were ancient Jewish texts, including fragments from books of the Hebrew Bible.

Over the next several years, ten more caves containing scrolls were discovered near the Dead Sea. In total, more than 900 scrolls were found, including fragments from the Hebrew Bible, other Jewish writings from the Second Temple period, and documents related to the history and beliefs of the Jewish community that produced and preserved the scrolls.

The discovery of the Dead Sea Scrolls has been called one of the most significant archaeological discoveries of the 20th century. They have played an essential role in the study of the Bible and the history of Judaism.[1]

## The Scrolls Acquisition

In 1947, the Bedouin shepherds who had discovered seven scrolls sold them to a local antiquities dealer, Khalil Iskander Shahin, also known as Kando. Kando arranged the sale of three scrolls to a Jewish scholar named Eleazar Sukenik, who recognized their historical and religious significance. Sukenik purchased the scrolls for the Hebrew University of Jerusalem.

The remaining four scrolls were sold to Metropolitan (i.e., bishop) Samuel, the Patriarch of the Syrian Orthodox Church in Jerusalem. Later, concerned that the scrolls may have been improperly obtained and needing to raise money for his church, Samuel offered them for sale in a Wall Street Journal advertisement in 1954.

In 1954, Yaegel Yadin, an Israeli archaeologist, military officer, politician, and the son of Eleazar Sukenik, arranged to purchase the remaining four scrolls on behalf of the State of Israel. Yadin negotiated the purchase with the help of an intermediary who acted as a go-between for the parties. The final four scrolls are housed along with the first three in Jerusalem's Shrine of the Book Museum.

**Picture 2**

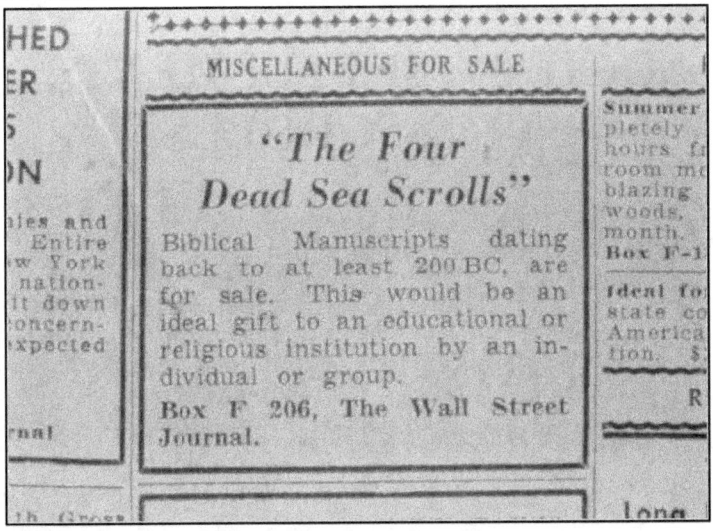

*Wall Street Journal Advertisement*, June 1, 1954
Leon Levy Dead Sea Scrolls Digital Library.
© Israel Antiquities Authority. Public Domain.
https://religionnews.com/wp-content/uploads/2017/10/WEB-DEAD-SEA-SCROLL-100517.jpg[2]

# PART ONE
# SOCIETY, SETTLEMENT, SITE & SCROLLS

# CHAPTER 1
# Society

## 1.1 Ancient World of the Scrolls

The ancient world of the scrolls was a time of great cultural and political upheaval in the Near East. It was marked by the presence of various empires and kingdoms in the region, such as the Roman Empire, the Ptolemaic Kingdom of Egypt, and the Seleucid Empire.

The Second Temple period in Jewish history lasted approximately 586 years (516 BCE – 70 CE). It began with the return to Zion (following the Babylonian exile) and the erection of the Second Temple. It concluded with the onset of the First Jewish-Roman War and the subsequent Roman destruction of Jerusalem and its temple in 70 CE.

The Second Temple was the center of Jewish religious and cultural life during this period and was an important site for the Jewish people.

This period is also referred to as the Intertestamental Period, the time between the completion of the Old Testament and the writing of the New Testament. The last book of the Old Testament, Malachi, was likely written in the 5th century BCE (400 BCE), and the first book of the New Testament, the Gospel of Mark, is estimated to have been written in the 1st century CE (around 70 CE). This time in history coincides precisely with what is often referred to as the Second Temple period.[3]

Judea, situated in the southern region of what is now Israel, holds historical importance as the namesake of the tribe of Judah, one of Israel's twelve tribes. It has been a pivotal area in Jewish history, encompassing much of the West Bank and portions of present-day Israel.

The West Bank includes many major cities and towns in ancient Judea, such as Bethlehem, Hebron, and Nablus. The State of Israel also includes parts of ancient Judea, including Jerusalem and the region around the Dead Sea.

The scrolls provide a unique glimpse into the cultural and religious practices of the Jewish people of the time, as well as the conflicts and tensions that existed between different groups. They also offer insights into the ancient world's broader social, political, and cultural context.

## 1.2 Historical Events and Period Rule

The era of the Dead Sea Scrolls extended from the third century Before the Common Era to the first century of the Common Era, marking a period characterized by notable political, cultural, and religious transformations in Judea. Numerous significant epochs of governance and occurrences unfolded throughout this era.

The Maccabean Revolt occurred in the 2nd century BCE, followed by the reign of the Hasmonean Dynasty from 140 BCE to 37 BCE.

The Herodian Dynasty ruled from 37 BCE to 92 CE, and Hellenism spread following Alexander the Great's death in 323

BCE until the rise of the Roman Empire in 31 BCE. These important events and periods of rule significantly influenced the development of Judaism and the broader region.

## *The Maccabean Revolt (167-160 BCE)*

According to traditional accounts, the Maccabean Revolt began in 167 BCE, when the Seleucid king Antiochus IV Epiphanes began a campaign to suppress Jewish religious practices and Hellenize the Jewish population of Palestine. The revolt ended in 160 BCE, when the Maccabees, led by Judah Maccabee, defeated the Seleucid army and established an independent Jewish state.

The Maccabees were victorious in their efforts and established the Hasmonean Dynasty, which ruled over Palestine for more than 100 years.[4]

## *Hasmonean Dynasty (140 BCE to 37 BCE)*

The Hasmonean dynasty was a Jewish dynasty that ruled over Palestine from 140 BCE to 37 BCE. The Maccabees founded the dynasty.

The Hasmoneans were a priestly family whose ancestry traces back to the tribe of Levi. They are known for their role in the Maccabean revolt. The Hasmoneans successfully established their kingdom and ruled over it for several generations.

The Hasmoneans are perhaps best known for their military victories over the Seleucid Empire, which allowed them to establish an independent Jewish state in Judea, and for their efforts to promote Jewish cultural and religious traditions. They are also remembered for modernizing and improving the infrastructure of their kingdom, including the construction of fortifications, roads, and aqueducts.

During the Hasmonean period, Palestine experienced a period of prosperity and relative stability, and the Hasmoneans are viewed as a successful and influential dynasty in Jewish history. However, towards the end of the Hasmonean period, the dynasty became weakened by internal strife and external threats. Forces of the Roman Republic conquered the Hasmonean kingdom in 63 BCE, and Herod the Great displaced the last reigning Hasmonean client-rulers in 37 BCE.[5]

### *Herodian Dynasty (37 BCE to 92 CE)*

The Herodian Dynasty was a Jewish dynasty that ruled over Palestine from 37 BCE to 92 CE. The dynasty originated with Herod the Great, who was designated as the ruler of Judea by the Roman Empire. The Herodian Dynasty was characterized by a blend of Jewish and Roman culture and was known for its efforts to modernize and improve the infrastructure of the kingdom. However, the Herodians were criticized by some Jews for collaborating with the Roman Empire and for a perceived lack of commitment to traditional Jewish values.

Herod was a controversial figure known for his ambitious building projects and brutal tactics. However, he was also a patron of the arts and a supporter of Jewish religious practices. The Herodians are remembered for their contributions to the development of Judea and their lasting impact on the cultural and political landscape of the region. The Herodians were also responsible for the expansion of the Second Temple in Jerusalem.

Despite controversies, the Herodian Dynasty played a vital role in the history of Palestine and the broader region of the ancient Near East.[6]

### *The Hellenistic Period (323 BCE to 31 BCE)*

The Hellenistic Era (323 BCE to 31 BCE) refers to the period characterized by the spread of Greek culture and intellectual pursuits that originated in ancient Greece and extended across the Mediterranean world.

Beginning with the passing of Alexander the Great in 323 BCE and lasting until the emergence of the Roman Empire in 31 BCE, this epoch witnessed the dissemination of Greek customs, language, and concepts throughout the area. During this time, interactions between Jews and Greek culture increased, leading to some Jewish individuals adopting aspects of Greek lifestyle and philosophy. Additionally, the Septuagint, a Greek translation of the Hebrew Bible widely utilized by Jews residing outside of Palestine, emerged during this era. The region was governed by a succession of Greek-speaking kingdoms, and many of the texts discovered in the Dead Sea Scrolls exhibit traces of Hellenistic influence.[7]

### *Roman Conquest of Palestine (63 BCE)*

The Roman conquest of Palestine occurred in 63 BCE when the Roman general Pompey defeated the Seleucid king Antiochus XIII and took control of Palestine. This event marked the end of Seleucid rule in Palestine and the beginning of Roman rule over the region.

During the Roman period, Palestine was ruled as a client state of the Roman Empire and governed by a series of Roman governors and later by the Herodian Dynasty, a Jewish dynasty that the Roman Empire appointed. The Roman conquest of Palestine had a significant impact on the history and culture of the region, as it introduced a new system of government and brought about significant changes in Palestine's political, social, and economic landscape.[8]

## *Rabbinic Judaism (1ˢᵗ Century CE)*

Rabbinic Judaism is a religious movement that emerged in Palestine during the early centuries of the Common Era. It is characterized by the belief in the centrality and authority of the Oral Torah, a body of teachings and interpretations of Jewish scripture that were transmitted orally from generation to generation. Rabbinic Judaism is also marked by a strong emphasis on studying Jewish law and tradition and the authority of the rabbis, who are considered the guardians and interpreters of Jewish law and custom.

During the Dead Sea Scrolls period, from the 3rd century BCE to the 1st century CE, various Jewish sects and movements emerged in Palestine, including the Pharisees and the Essenes. These groups are believed to have produced many of the texts found among the Dead Sea Scrolls and influenced Rabbinic Judaism's development.

Rabbinic Judaism began to take shape during the late 1st century CE after the Second Temple in Jerusalem was destroyed in 70 CE. This also marked the end of the temple-based system of Jewish worship and practice. During this period, Jewish religious leaders developed a system of study and interpretation of Jewish scripture and tradition that would later become the basis of Rabbinic Judaism.

Rabbinic Judaism continued to evolve over the next few centuries. It became the dominant form of Judaism in the Jewish dispersion following the expulsion of the Jews from Palestine in 135 CE. Today, the majority of Jews around the world practice Rabbinic Judaism.[9]

### *The Rise of Christianity & the Early Church (1ˢᵗ Century CE)*

Christianity emerged as a distinct religion during the 1st century CE. The early Christian movement was a Jewish sect that emerged in Palestine during the Roman period and spread rapidly throughout the Roman Empire and beyond.

As described in the New Testament, Jesus of Nazareth was a Jewish teacher crucified by the Roman authorities in Jerusalem around 30 CE. However, his followers believed that he was the Messiah (or Christ) prophesied in Jewish scripture and that he had risen from the dead. Therefore, they began to spread his teachings and message throughout Palestine and the Roman Empire.

During the Dead Sea Scrolls period, the early Christian movement and the development of the early Church was shaped by a number of significant events and figures. Among them was the Apostle Paul, who played a key role in spreading Christianity to non-Jewish individuals, and the Apostle Peter, who is considered the first pope by Catholics. The early Church faced significant challenges, including persecution from Roman authorities and conflicts with other Jewish sects over issues of doctrine and practice. In spite of these challenges, the early Church grew and spread, eventually becoming a major force in the history of the ancient world.

The early Christian movement faced significant challenges and persecution from Jewish and Roman authorities, but it continued to grow and spread. By the 4th century CE, Christianity was dominating the Roman Empire, and it continues to be one of the world's major religions to this day.[10]

**Table 1**

| Ancient Political and Military Events ||
|---|---|
| 198 BCE | Seleucid rule over Judea begins |
| 168 BCE | Hasmonean revolt |
| 164 BCE | Temple purified by Judas Maccabeus |
| 63 BCE | Rome occupies Jerusalem |
| 37 BCE | Herod the Great conquers Jerusalem |
| 6 BCE - 41 CE | Judea placed under procurators (Roman treasury officers) |
| 44-66 CE | Procurators rule |
| 66 CE | Revolt against Rome |
| 68 CE | Roman legions destroy the Qumran settlement |
| 70 CE | Roman legions conquer Jerusalem and destroy the Temple |
| 73 CE | Masada falls to Rome |

Source: Modified from the *"The Dead Sea Scrolls,"* Ellen Middlebrook Herron, ed. 2003.[11]

*Bar Kokhba Revolt (132 CE to 135 CE)*

    The Bar Kokhba revolt was a military conflict in Judea (modern-day Israel) in the 2nd century CE. It was led by a Jewish leader named Simon bar Kokhba, who spearheaded a rebellion against the Roman Empire.

    The revolt began in 132 CE after the Roman Emperor Hadrian announced plans to build a temple to Jupiter on the site of the temple in Jerusalem and to rename Judea Syria to Palaestina. This move insulted the Jews, who considered

Jerusalem their holy city, and sparked a widespread rebellion against Roman rule.

Bar Kokhba and his followers, known as the Sicarii, fought against the Romans for three years, and the revolt was eventually put down in 135 CE. However, the Romans responded to the rebellion with great force, killing many Jews and destroying much of the region. The revolt's aftermath was devastating for the Jews, who were exiled from Jerusalem and lost much of their land and wealth.

Although the Bar Kokhba revolt took place after the period when the Dead Sea Scrolls were produced and the Qumran community was active, it is still relevant to the study of the Dead Sea Scrolls as it occurred in the same region and involved many of the same groups of people. The revolt is also significant because it played a role in the development of early Judaism and the relationship between the Jews and the Roman Empire.[12]

## 1.3 Near East Jewish Religious Sects

The Dead Sea Scrolls provide important insights into Jewish sects and movements that were active during the period. Four of the primary sects that were prominent during the time of the Dead Sea Scrolls were the Essenes, Sadducees, Pharisees, and Zealots.

**Essenes:** The Essenes were a Jewish sectarian group living in the Judean Desert near the Dead Sea and are believed to have been the scribes who copied and preserved many of the Dead Sea Scrolls.

They were a separatist group that lived a communal and ascetic lifestyle in the desert near the Dead Sea and various other locales. They were opposed to the temple in Jerusalem and the mainstream Jewish leadership and believed in the imminent arrival of a messianic age. They were known for their strict adherence to the laws of purity and strict communal discipline.[13]

According to ancient sources, the Essenes were a celibate, communal group that lived a simple and austere lifestyle. They were known for their commitment to religious study and the practice of regular ritual immersion in water. The Essenes are mentioned in several ancient sources, including the writings of the Jewish historian Josephus and the Roman historian Pliny the Elder.

**Sadducees:** The Sadducees were a wealthy and influential Jewish sect closely associated with the temple in Jerusalem and the mainstream Jewish leadership. They were known for their strict adherence to the written laws of the Torah. They opposed the Pharisees, who believed in the authority of oral tradition, and the Essenes, who rejected the temple and the mainstream Jewish leadership.

The Sadducees were primarily comprised of Jewish priests and aristocrats who rejected oral tradition and the concept of an afterlife. They were generally more conservative in their beliefs and practices than the Pharisees.[14]

**Pharisees:** The Pharisees were a Jewish sect largely comprised of scholars and religious leaders who emphasized the importance of oral tradition and the interpretation of Jewish law. They opposed the Sadducees and the Essenes and were more popular among the general Jewish population. The New Testament mentions the Pharisees as being opposed to Jesus and his teachings. They believed in the resurrection of the dead and the existence of an afterlife and were influential in the development of Rabbinic Judaism.[15]

**Zealots:** The Zealots were a Jewish nationalist movement that sought to resist Roman rule and reclaim Jewish independence. They were known for their willingness to use violent means to achieve their goals and were opposed to collaborating with the Romans. The Zealots are mentioned in the New Testament as being opposed to Jesus and his teachings. They were known for their militancy and were active in the First Jewish-Roman War (66-70 CE).[16]

It is important to note that these four sects were not the only groups within Judaism during this period, and there were many other sects and movements with their own beliefs and practices. The Dead Sea Scrolls provide essential insights into the beliefs and practices of these groups and the broader Jewish community during this period.

# CHAPTER 2
# Settlement

## 2.1 Theories of the Qumran Sect

There are several theories about the Qumran sect, a Jewish sectarian group that lived in the area of the Dead Sea in the 2nd century BCE and the 1st century CE. The group is best known for the Dead Sea Scrolls.

1. One theory is that the Qumran sect was a group of Essenes. The Essenes were a Jewish religious movement mentioned in ancient sources such as the writings of the historian Josephus. The Essenes are believed to have lived a communal, ascetic lifestyle and followed strict rules for religious practice. Many scholars believe that the Qumran sect and the Essenes were the same and that its members wrote some of the Dead Sea Scrolls.[17]

2. Another theory is that the Qumran sect was a group of Sadducees. The Sadducees were a wealthy and influential group known for their strict adherence to the traditional laws and practices of Judaism. According to this theory, the Qumran sect was a group of Sadducees who left mainstream Judaism and formed a community in the wilderness.[18]

3. The third theory is that Qumran was a military outpost. According to this theory, the Qumran community was not

a religious group but a military installation used to protect the region from foreign invaders.

4. The fourth theory is that Qumran was a vacation vista, a place wealthy Jews could go to relieve themselves of the heat and humidity of the lowlands. According to this theory, the Qumran community was a resort or vacation spot used by wealthy Jews.

For this book, we will align with scholars' widely held belief that the Qumran sect was a group of Essenes, although we acknowledge that the sect may have been influenced by other groups as well. The true nature and purpose of the Qumran sect remain a topic of debate among experts in the field. It is worth noting that these theories are not mutually exclusive and that the Qumran community may have been a blend of various influences.

## 2.2 Khirbet Qumran

Khirbet Qumran (Khirbet is the Arabic word for "ruin") is an ancient archeological site near the Dead Sea in the Judean Desert in Israel. It is situated on a dry marl plateau, located about 1.5 km (0.9 miles) from the northwestern shore of the Dead Sea, about 10 km (6 miles) south of Jericho, and about 50 km (31 miles) southeast of Jerusalem. The nearest modern-day community to Khirbet Qumran is the Palestinian village of Ain Fashkha, located approximately 1 km (0.6 miles) to the northwest of the site. Several other Palestinian villages found in the vicinity include Al-Sawahira ash-Sharqiyya, Al-Auja, and Ein Gedi.

Picture 3                    Picture 4

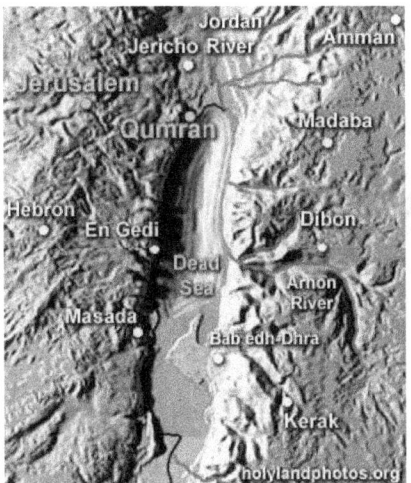 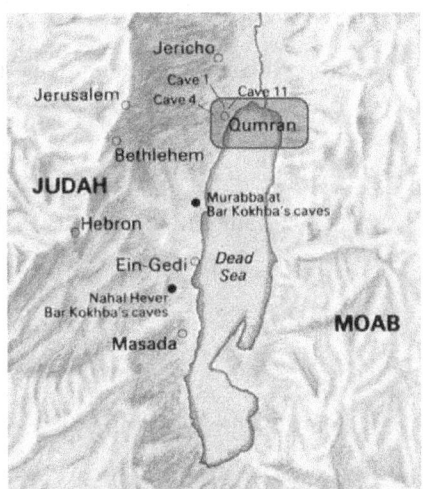

**Qumran Region Aerial Image**      **Qumran Region Map**
http://holylandphotos.org           https://www.johnpratt.com/items

The Qumran site contains features consistent with the description of an Essene monastery, including a large communal dining room, a scriptorium (a room where texts were copied), a cemetery, and ritual baths. The settlement also had a system of cisterns and channels for collecting and storing water, which was important in the desert environment. It is thought that about 200 people lived there at any given time.

The settlement at Qumran was discovered in the early 20th century and was first excavated in 1951 by an Israeli archaeologist named Roland de Vaux. Since then, the site has been the subject of ongoing excavations and research. It has provided insight into the lives of the Qumran sect, likely the Essenes, and the cultural and religious context in which the Dead Sea Scrolls were produced.[19]

The excavations revealed that Qumran was principally in use from the Hasmonean times until sometime after the temple's destruction in Jerusalem in 70 CE. De Vaux divided this use into three periods (not including the period of very early occupancy), which include periods Ia and Ib of early and latter Hasmonean times, period II during the Herodian era, and period III of Roman re-occupancy. The site was believed to have been vacant for about 34 years after an earthquake in 31 BCE.

**Table 2**

| Qumran Occupancy Periods | | |
|---|---|---|
| **Early Israelite Period** | 8th - 7th century BCE | Pre-Essene occupancy |
| **Period Ia** | 130-100 BCE | During the time of Hasmonean leader John Hyrcanus |
| **Period Ib** | 100-31 BCE | Latter Hasmonean until the earthquake and fire |
| **Unoccupied** | 31 BCE-4 CE | Break in occupation after the earthquake in 31 BCE |
| **Period II** | 4 BCE - 68 CE | The Herodian Era, up to the destruction by the Romans during the Jewish War in 68 CE |
| **Period III** | 68-90 CE | Brief reoccupation by the Romans |

Source: Modified from the "*The Dead Sea Scrolls,*" Ellen Middlebrook Herron, ed. 2003.[20]

The ruins at Khirbet Qumran consist of the remains of several buildings. The site that de Vaux first uncovered divides into two main sections: the main building, a square structure of two stories featuring a central courtyard and a defensive tower on its northwestern corner, and a secondary building to the west. The excavation revealed a complex water system that supplied water to a few stepped cisterns, some quite large, located in several parts of the site. Two of these cisterns were within the main building.[21]

The buildings and the water system show signs of evolution throughout the life of the settlement, with frequent additions, improvements, and extensions. The water channel appears to have been raised to carry water to newer cisterns farther away, and a dam was placed in the upper section of Wadi (riverbed) Qumran to secure water brought to the site by an aqueduct. Rooms were added, floors were raised, pottery ovens relocated, and locations repurposed.

De Vaux found three inkwells at Qumran, and over the following years, more inkwells with a Qumran origin became known, bringing the total to six. These are more inkwells than were found at any other site during the Second Temple period, a significant indication of writing at Qumran.

Today, Qumran is a popular tourist destination open to the public. The Israel Nature and Parks Authority manages the site.[22]

**Picture 5**

***Khirbet Qumran*** is an archaeological site in the West Bank located on a dry plateau about a mile from the northwestern shore of the Dead Sea. Public Domain.
https://fundacioncarf.org/en/the-historical-figure-of-jesus/

## 2.3 Artifacts

The excavation of Khirbet Qumran and the Dead Sea caves has revealed numerous artifacts that provide context for the settlement. These artifacts include coins, pottery, human remains and graves, and objects related to religious practices. By analyzing these artifacts and the graves' contents, we can better understand the Qumran sect and their way of life. Together, these artifacts help to paint a more complete picture of the Qumran community.

*Coins*

Coins ranging in date from the 4th century BCE to the 1st century CE were found at the Qumran site, with the majority of coins dating to the later period of Qumran's occupation.

The coins found at Qumran include various types and denominations, including Greek and Roman coins. Some of the most commonly found coins at the site are Roman denarii, the main Roman silver coin used for everyday transactions during that period, and sestertii and dupondii, larger bronze denominations.

In addition to Roman coins, many Greek coins were found at Qumran. These include silver tetradrachms and drachmas, used in the Hellenistic period, and smaller bronze coins known as obols and lepta.

At the time of the excavation of Khirbet Qumran in the early 1950s, the most prized find was three small ceramic vessels containing over five hundred silver coins. These were found buried under a doorway on the west side of the monastery. The coins were minted at various times in the late second and first centuries BCE.

The presence of these coins at Qumran suggests that the settlement had some level of interaction with the broader world and was not entirely isolated. The coins also provide information about the chronology of the site and the economic activities that took place there.[23]

**Pictures 6**

(l) *Scroll Jar*. A large number of ceramic cylindrical scroll jars were found at Qumran. Utilitarian items found in Qumran include small jugs, flasks, drinking cups, cooking pots, serving dishes, and bowls.
© Israel Antiquities Authority. Public Domain.
https://www.loc.gov/exhibits/scrolls/art2.html

(r) *Coins*. In 1955, three intact ceramic vessels containing 561 silver coins dating between 136 and 10 BCE were found under a doorway at the Qumran excavation site.
© Israel Antiquities Authority.
https://www.loc.gov/exhibits/scrolls/art2.html

### *Pottery*

Pottery is a common artifact found at the Qumran site, providing valuable information about the history and occupation of the settlement. The pottery found at Qumran ranges from the 4th century BCE to the 1st century CE, with the majority of pottery dating to the later period of Qumran's occupation.

The pottery can give us an idea of the types of activities that took place at the settlement and the cultural influences and trade connections of the people who lived there.

The pottery found at Qumran includes a variety of types and styles, including vessels for cooking, serving, and storing food, lamps, figurines, and other decorative objects. One of the most common types of pottery found at Qumran is cooking and serving vessels, such as pots, jugs, and bowls. These vessels would have been used in the preparation and consumption of food. The pottery also includes storage vessels, such as jars and amphorae, which would have served for preserving and storing food and other goods.[24]

***Cemetery***

The primary cemetery at Qumran is located east of the settlement and contains up to 1,200 burial graves. The cemetery was most likely used from the 2nd century BCE all the way to the 1st century CE by the members of the Qumran sect.

The cemetery is divided into six sections: the primary cemetery and its extensions, the north cemetery, and the south cemetery. Although the Qumran cemetery has many graves, only 53 were excavated, as excavating cemeteries is forbidden under Jewish law. It is important to note that several female remains were found among the excavated graves.

The cemetery at the Qumran site is known for the unique characteristics of its graves, which differ from each other in various ways; some graves show characteristics associated with one tradition, while others show characteristics associated with another tradition.

Most graves are oriented with the head towards the south and the feet towards the north, although some graves in the southern extension of the primary cemetery are oriented east and west.

The graves at Qumran are marked by piles of fieldstones arranged in an oval shape, with some graves featuring larger stones at the head or feet. The graves are dug straight down to a depth of between 0.8 and 2.5 meters, at the bottom of which is a small cavity where the body is placed. A stone or clay brick cap protects the body, which is typically laid on its back, alone or with another body.

There are several theories about the bodies buried in the Qumran cemetery, with some suggesting that the primary section of the cemetery may be from the Second Temple period and that one or more of the extensions may be from a later medieval period. Some bodies at Qumran were buried with minimal possessions, such as pottery or jewelry, while others were buried with no possessions.

The differing orientation of the graves, the presence or absence of possessions, and the female remains suggest either changes in burial practices over time or the fact that different groups of people used the cemetery at different times.

The origins of the bodies buried in the Qumran cemetery are still the subject of ongoing research and investigation.[25]

## *Other Items Discovered*

Tefillin, mezuzah, ostraca, and ossuaries are all related to Jewish religious practices of the time, and these artifacts were discovered at Khirbet Qumran and nearby caves.

**Tefillin** are small leather boxes containing parchment scrolls with passages from the Hebrew Bible written on them. Observant Jews wear them during morning prayers to show devotion to God.

**Mezuzah** is a small parchment scroll containing the same passages from the Hebrew Bible that are found in tefillin. It is placed in a small decorative case and then affixed to the doorpost of a Jewish home as a reminder of the importance of observing the commandments of God.

**Ostraca** are pieces of pottery or stone inscribed with writing, often used as a form of informal communication or record keeping. In Jewish history, ostraca have been found with Hebrew inscriptions and are thought to have been used for various purposes, such as official documents or personal letters.

**Ossuaries** are small chambers or containers that store human bones, typically after the flesh has decomposed.

The discovery of these objects at Khirbet Qumran and in the Dead Sea caves signifies that the region has a long history of Jewish habitation and religious activity. The Dead Sea region was home to many Jewish communities during ancient times, and these communities likely used these objects to practice their religion.[26]

# CHAPTER 3
# Site

## 3.1 The Dead Sea Scroll Caves

The Dead Sea Scrolls were discovered in stages over nine years, from 1947 to 1956, revealing manuscripts and artifacts that had been hidden for nearly two millennia. In this section, a very brief overview of each cave is presented.

*Cave 1*

Cave One was discovered by a Bedouin shepherd chasing a stray in 1947. It was likely a place to hide and secure writings for the future. The seven scrolls discovered in this cave were the Manual of Discipline, War of Sons of Light, Thanksgiving Scroll, Isaiah A and B, Genesis Apocryphon, and Habakkuk Commentary.[27]

*Cave 2*

Cave Two was discovered in 1952 and is one of the smaller caves where the Dead Sea Scrolls were found. Thirty-three fragmentary scrolls were unearthed in this cave.

*Cave 3*

The Copper Scroll, found in this cave in 1952, lists 64 treasures hidden in the Judean wilderness and Jerusalem area. This scroll was the only one photographed in situ. It is displayed in the Jordan Museum.[28]

**Picture 7**

***Qumran Caves Aerial Views.*** The caves where the scrolls were located were embedded in the upper cliffs and the lower marl terraces above the shore of the Dead Sea, within a few hundred yards and 1.5 km from Khirbet Qumran. The Leon Levy Dead Sea Scrolls Digital Library. © Israel Antiquities Authority
https://www.itsgila.com/highlightsqumran.htm
https://www.deadseascrolls.org.il/learn-about-the-scrolls/discovery-and-publication

### *Cave 4*

Discovered in 1952 by the Bedouin, Cave Four is the most famous of the Dead Sea Scroll caves and is the most significant in terms of finds. More than 15,000 fragments from over 600 manuscripts were found in this cave. The scrolls in this cave were poorly preserved as they were not stored in jars but appeared to have been laid flat on shelves.

Given its immediate proximity to the Qumran settlement and considering how the scrolls were kept, Cave Four most likely served as a library for the Qumran sect.

*Cave 5*

Archaeologists discovered this eroded cave in the marl terrace close to the site of Qumran. Fragments of 26 scrolls were found in this cave.[29]

*Cave 6*

This cave contained 31 scroll fragments and is the most accessible of the Dead Sea Scroll caves to Qumran visitors today.[30]

**Picture 8**

***Cave 4 Interior.*** This cave likely served as a library for the inhabitants of Qumran and was filled with wooden shelves. Note the holes in the cave walls used to hold shelf brackets.
© Bibleplaces.com. Public Domain.
https://www.goodnews.ie/qumranarticle.shtml

*Cave 7*

Everything found in cave seven was written in Greek. The cave appears to have collapsed sometime after the scrolls were hidden.[31]

*Cave 8*

Archaeologists discovered fragments of Genesis and Psalms, a mezuzah, and dozens of squares of small leather strips. Workers who may have lived there were possibly involved in making these strips.[32]

*Cave 9*

Discovered in 1952, Cave 9 was carved into the southern part of the Qumran plateau. It is one of the only caves accessible by passing through the settlement at Qumran. Only one fragment was found in this cave.

*Cave 10*

Only one ostracon (a piece of pottery or stone inscribed with writing) was found in Cave 10.

*Cave 11*

The Bedouin discovered it in 1956. It was the last cave discovered at the time and produced the last scrolls. Thirty-two fragmentary scrolls were found, including the nearly complete Temple Scroll.[33]

*Cave 12*

In February 2017, researchers from Hebrew University in Jerusalem, Israel, and Liberty University in Virginia, USA, while excavating near Khirbet Qumran, discovered a cave believed to have once housed ancient scrolls. Inside Cave 12, they uncovered numerous storage jars and lids dating back to the Second Temple period. They were carefully concealed within niches along the cave walls and deep inside a lengthy tunnel at its rear. All the jars had been shattered and their contents were missing. Additionally, fragments of materials used to wrap scrolls, a twine employed for tying scrolls, and a processed leather fragment, presumably from a scroll, were discovered in this cave.

In addition, a pair of iron pickaxe heads dating from the 1950s was discovered, suggesting that the cave had been previously looted.[34]

Table 3

| Number of Scrolls Represented by Site Fragments Found ||
|---|---:|
| Qumran, Cave 4 | 666 |
| Qumran, Cave 1 | 80 |
| Qumran, Cave 2 | 33 |
| Qumran, Cave 11 | 32 |
| Qumran, Cave 6 | 31 |
| Qumran, Cave 5 | 26 |
| Qumran, Cave 7 | 24 |
| Qumran, Cave 3 | 15 |
| Qumran, Cave 8 | 5 |
| Qumran, Cave 9 | 1 |
| **Total Scrolls** | **913** |

Source: Modified from *The Leon Levy Dead Sea Scrolls Digital Library,* Israel Antiquities Authority. https://www.deadseascrolls.org.il

*Cave Summary*

A total of twelve Qumran caves have been studied, with many being discovered by Bedouins. The exceptions are Caves 3, 5, 7, 8, 9, 10, and 12, which archaeologists found. It is estimated that there may have been as many as 30-40 caves in the marl terrace at one time.

The scrolls found in these caves have revealed that every book of the Old Testament is represented in them (except for Esther) and that no New Testament books or fragments were found. Complete scrolls were only discovered in Caves 1, 3, and 11.

The largest number of fragments found were from the following books: Psalms (36 copies), Deuteronomy (30 copies), Enoch (25), Isaiah (21), Jubilees (21), and Genesis (20 copies). A full list is found in Chapter Eight, Table 7.

After being hidden for nearly 2000 years, the caves of Qumran have provided a wealth of knowledge about the Qumran sect and the wider ancient world. The Dead Sea Scrolls discovered in these caves have significantly impacted our understanding of the ancient Near East's history and culture, the evolution of Judaism, and the emergence of Christianity.

## 3.2 More Sites in the Judean Desert

Masada, Wadi Marraba'at (also known as Murabba'at), Nahal Hever, Nahal Se'elim, and Wadi Daliyeh are all archaeological sites in Israel and the West Bank that scholars have excavated and studied. These sites have unique histories and significance, and some have contributed to the corpus of the Dead Sea Scrolls texts.[35]

**Masada**, a renowned palace and fortress compound situated atop a rugged plateau in the Judean Desert, stands out. Originally constructed by King Herod the Great in the 1st century BCE, it later served as a stronghold for Jewish insurgents, known as the Zealots, during the First Jewish-Roman War. Masada is well-known for the heroic stand of the Jewish rebels against the Romans, who besieged the fortress in 73 CE. The site has been extensively excavated and is now a popular tourist destination. Eight scroll fragments that can be affiliated with the Dead Sea Scroll collection were discovered there.

**Wadi Marraba'at** is an archaeological site located on the West Bank. It is believed to have been a Jewish settlement during the Second Temple period. The site includes structures, including a synagogue, and has yielded numerous artifacts such as coins, pottery, and stone vessels. Six scroll fragments associated with the Dead Sea Scroll collection were found there.

**Nahal Hever** is an archaeological site located in the Judean Desert. It is best known for the discovery of the Cave of Letters, which contained a number of important documents from the Second Temple period, including letters, legal documents, and fragments of the Hebrew Bible. Five scroll fragments affiliated with the Dead Sea Scroll collection were discovered there.

**Nahal Se'elim** is an archaeological site located in the Negev Desert. It is believed to have been a settlement during the Roman and Byzantine periods, and the site has yielded pottery, coins, and inscriptions.

**Wadi Daliyeh** is an archaeological site located in the Jordan Valley. It is believed to have been a settlement during the Iron Age, and the site has yielded important artifacts, including inscriptions and seals.

These sites provide valuable information about the region's history and culture and are important sources for understanding the historical context.[36]

# CHAPTER 4
# Scrolls Creation and Evaluation
## 4.1 Languages and Scripts

The Dead Sea Scrolls texts are primarily written in three languages: Hebrew, Aramaic, and Greek.

**Hebrew:** The vast majority of the scrolls, particularly many of the biblical manuscripts, are in Hebrew, underscoring its role as the sacred and scholarly language of the Jewish people during that period.

Hebrew is a Semitic language that is the national language of Israel and one of the official languages of the State of Palestine. It is the language of the Jewish people, spoken by millions around the world. The Hebrew language has a long and rich history and has played a central role in Jewish culture and religion for centuries. Many of the oldest Dead Sea Scrolls are written in Hebrew, providing insight into ancient Israel's language, literature, and culture.

**Aramaic:** Aramaic was widely spoken in the region during the Second Temple era, so it is logical that a notable portion of the scrolls are in this language. These include scriptural texts, apocryphal literature, and sectarian documents.

Aramaic is a Semitic language spoken throughout the ancient Near East and is still spoken today by many people. It was the region's dominant language during the time of the Dead Sea Scrolls and was widely used in the Roman Empire. The Dead Sea

Scrolls include texts written in both Eastern and Western Aramaic, providing important insights into the history and development of the language. Scrolls written in Aramaic tend to be newer than those written in Hebrew.

**Greek:** A smaller quantity of the scrolls is written in Greek, encompassing some biblical texts, which indicates the Hellenistic cultural influence in the area.

Greek is an Indo-European language spoken throughout the Mediterranean in ancient times. It was the language of the Greek Empire and was widely spoken and written in the Roman Empire. A small number of the Dead Sea Scrolls are written in Greek, providing important insights into the use of the language in the region during this period. Scrolls written in Greek are some of the newest of the Dead Sea Scrolls, often originating from the 1st century CE.

**Other languages:** A very limited number of scrolls are found in other languages, highlighting that Hebrew, Aramaic, and Greek were the principal languages at the time the scrolls were written.

**Table 4**

| Languages of the Scrolls | |
|---|---|
| Hebrew | **80-85%** |
| Aramaic | **15-17%** |
| Greek | **2-3%** |
| Other (Latin, Nabatean, Unidentified) | **<1%** |

Produced by the author using multiple sources as resource material.

While there might be slight variations in the exact percentages depending on the source, the distribution provided is broadly accurate and reflects the consensus among scholars. The Dead Sea Scrolls are a valuable source of information about the ancient Near East's languages, literature, and culture. They have significantly impacted the study of these subjects.

## 4.2 Scribes

The majority of scholarly opinion is that the Qumran sect of Essenes wrote a significant portion of the scrolls to preserve their religious traditions and teachings. It also holds that other Jewish scholars and scribes, who were not necessarily members of the Qumran community but shared similar beliefs and practices, wrote a substantial portion of the scrolls. These scribes may have been part of a larger network of Jewish scholars concerned with preserving Jewish tradition and knowledge.

While it is difficult to determine who the scribes of the Dead Sea Scrolls were, when scrolls are compared, it appears that very few scrolls have been written by the same scribe.

We may never know the true circumstances surrounding the creation and preservation of the texts. While it will remain a matter of debate, the truth is likely a combination of various theories.[37]

## 4.3 Dating the Scrolls

Over the years, various techniques have been deployed to date the Dead Sea Scrolls. These have included paleography, carbon-14, archeological and historical context, ink and materials, and DNA.

- **Paleography:** This involves examining the handwriting and style of the scrolls to determine when they were written.
- **Carbon dating:** This entails assessing the quantity of carbon-14, a radioactive form of carbon, within the scrolls to ascertain their age.
- **Historical and Archaeological context:** This involves examining the artifacts and other materials found with the scrolls and the events and people mentioned in the texts to determine their date.
- **Ink and Material:** This involves examining the ingredients and techniques used to make the ink and assessing the quality and condition of the parchment to determine when a scroll was written.
- **DNA:** This involves analyzing the DNA of the parchment to determine the species of animal from which it was made and provide insights into the environment and climate in which the animal lived.

Overall, dating the Dead Sea Scrolls is a complex process involving multiple techniques and requiring the expertise of a range of specialists. The following is additional detail on these dating methodologies.

## *Dating with Paleography*

Paleography is the study of handwriting and the style of written documents. It is one of the techniques used to date the Dead Sea Scrolls. By examining the handwriting, the style of the script, and the type of ink and parchment used, paleographers can often determine when a document was written.

One of the key features of paleography is the identification of different scripts and handwriting styles used at different times in history. For example, the scrolls contain a variety of scripts, including Hebrew, Aramaic, and Greek, and these scripts changed over time as the languages evolved. By examining these features, paleographers can often determine the general time in which a scroll was written, even if they cannot pinpoint the exact date.

In the case of the Dead Sea Scrolls, paleography has been used to establish that they were written over a period of several centuries, with the earliest scrolls dating back to the 3rd century BCE and the latest scrolls dating back to the 1st century CE. However, paleography is only one of the techniques used to date the scrolls, and the exact dates of the scrolls are still the subject of ongoing research and debate.[38]

## *Carbon-14 Dating*

Carbon-14 dating has been used to date many of the Dead Sea Scrolls. The findings from these investigations have offered significant insights into the scrolls' age. In general, the carbon-14 dating results have confirmed the dates suggested by other methods, such as paleography, but there have been some discrepancies between the results of different studies.

One of the challenges of using carbon-14 dating to date the Dead Sea Scrolls is that the carbon-14 content of the parchment (animal skin) used to write the scrolls could be affected by several factors. For example, the age of the animal from which the parchment was made, the environment in which it lived, and the methods used to prepare and preserve the parchment can all affect the carbon-14 content of the parchment.

In addition, the carbon-14 content of the ink used to write the scrolls could also be affected by the ingredients used to make the ink and the methods used to preserve it. These factors can introduce uncertainty into the carbon-14 dating results, and it is important to carefully take into account these aspects when analyzing the findings of carbon-14 dating research on the Dead Sea Scrolls.[39]

### *Historical and Archaeological Context*

Dating the Dead Sea Scrolls using historical and archaeological context involves examining the events and figures mentioned in the scrolls and the artifacts and materials found with them to determine when they were written.

The approach to dating the scrolls using historical context is to examine the events and people mentioned in the texts and compare them to known historical events and figures. By comparing the references in the scrolls to these known historical events and figures, researchers can narrow down the possible period in which the scrolls were written.

Another approach is to examine the artifacts and materials found with the scrolls, such as coins, pottery, and other objects, to determine their date. By examining the style and characteristics of these artifacts, researchers can often determine when they were made and use this information to help date the scrolls.

### *Dating with Ink and Material*

In addition to previously mentioned dating methodologies, the materials used to write the Dead Sea Scrolls, such as the type of ink and parchment, can help date the scrolls.

The ink used to write the scrolls was made from various substances, including carbon-based materials like lampblack and soot and metallic substances like iron gall. The specific ingredients and techniques used to make the ink can vary depending on the time and location in which the scrolls were written. By examining the ingredients and techniques used to make the ink, researchers can often determine when a scroll was written.

The parchment (animal skin) used to write the scrolls can also provide clues about their age. The quality and condition of the parchment can differ based on the age of the creature from which it was made, as well as the methods used to prepare and preserve it. By examining the quality and condition of the parchment, researchers can often determine when a scroll was written.

### *Dating with DNA*

DNA analysis has not been used extensively to determine the date of the scrolls, as DNA is a fragile molecule that is prone to degradation over time and is generally not well preserved in ancient manuscripts.

However, DNA analysis has been used to study the origin and evolution of the animals from which the parchment (animal skin) used to write the Dead Sea Scrolls was made. DNA analysis is not a primary method for dating the Dead Sea Scrolls and is generally used in conjunction with other techniques, such as paleography and carbon dating.[40]

## 4.4 Reconstructing

Reconstructing the Dead Sea Scrolls from the thousands of fragments that were discovered was and is a complex and time-consuming task, although the scrolls' digitization has made it easier. Reconstructing the scrolls involves several different steps.

- **Sorting and cataloging:** The first step in reconstructing the scrolls is to sort and catalog the fragments according to their size, shape, and content. This process helps to identify which fragments belong to the same scroll and can be pieced together.
- **Cleaning and preservation:** Many of the fragments were damaged or covered in dirt and grime when they were discovered, so they must be carefully cleaned and preserved

to prevent further deterioration. This typically involves using various techniques, including careful brushing, washing, and drying.

- **Piecing together the fragments:** Once the fragments have been sorted and cleaned, they can be pieced together like a puzzle to reassemble the remains of the original scroll. This process is typically done by aligning the edges of the fragments and matching the handwriting and other features.
- **Translation and interpretation:** Once a scroll has been reconstructed, it must be translated and interpreted to understand its content. Scholars who are experts in the languages and cultures of ancient Judaism typically accomplish this.

Reconstructing the Dead Sea Scrolls is challenging, and it is not uncommon for it to take many years or even decades to fully reconstruct a single scroll. However, reconstructing the scrolls is an important part of the ongoing efforts to understand and preserve this unique and invaluable part of human history.[41]

## 4.5 Cataloging the Scrolls

The Dead Sea Scrolls are identified and cataloged by a standard reference system that includes:

1. The cave number where the manuscript was discovered (if there were multiple caves at a site yielding manuscripts)

2. The name of the site where it was found (e.g., Q = Qumran, Mur = Wadi Murabbaʻat, Masada, Nahal Hever)
3. The identification number of the scroll for that site or the manuscript's name that describes its contents.

For example, 4Q52 (a.k.a. 4QSamuelb) was found in cave four at Qumran, and it holds the position of 52nd in the list of scrolls published from this cave. A title with superscripted "b" indicates that this is the second listed copy of Samuel's books from this cave.[42]

**Picture 9**

The "Scrollery." The Scroll Room at the Rockefeller Museum (formerly the Palestine Archaeological Museum) in East Jerusalem. Public Domain.
https://www.newhistorian.com/2016/10/15/25-dead-sea-scroll-fragments/

# PART TWO
# UNDERSTANDING AND UNVEILING THE SCROLLS

# CHAPTER 5
# Editorial Process and Publication
## 5.1 The Scrolls Editorial Team

The original Dead Sea Scrolls editorial team, known as the International Team, was formed in the 1950s and consisted of eight scholars responsible for overseeing the publication of the scrolls. The team was composed of four Catholic scholars and four Protestant scholars. Father Jean Starcky, a Catholic scholar of Semitic languages, led it, and the Rockefeller Foundation funded the International Team from 1955 to 1960.

The team was responsible for overseeing the publication of the scrolls and coordinating the efforts of the many scholars involved in studying and translating the texts. Every member of the team possessed a distinct realm of specialized knowledge and was responsible for overseeing the work of the scholars working in that area. For example, Father Starcky was responsible for overseeing the publication of specific biblical texts written in Hebrew and Aramaic. At the same time, another member of the team, Professor Paul Kahle, was responsible for overseeing the publication of texts written in Greek. The team also included experts in other areas, such as paleography, linguistics, and archaeology, who were responsible for providing guidance and expertise on interpreting the texts.

The publication of the scrolls has been a complex and controversial process, and the original editorial team, composed of scholars from various disciplines and countries, faced criticism for its lack of Jewish representation. Some have argued the absence of Jewish scholars on the team contributed to an incomplete or biased understanding of the scrolls and their significance and that the team's interpretation of the scrolls was influenced by the political and cultural context of the time. In recent years, efforts have been made to address these criticisms and to include a more diverse group of scholars in the publication and interpretation of the scrolls.

Overall, the work of the original editorial team of the Dead Sea Scrolls was essential to the ongoing efforts to understand and interpret these important historical texts. Despite the many challenges and difficulties they faced, the team made significant progress in the study and publication of the scrolls, and their work has contributed significantly to our understanding of the history and culture of ancient Judaism.[43]

## 5.2 Challenges and Delays

The original International Team faced a number of challenges and delays in their efforts to publish and study the scrolls. Some of these challenges included:

**Access to the scrolls:** One of the main challenges faced by the editorial team was that they did not have unrestricted access to all the scrolls. Many of the scrolls were held in private collections or were in possession of the Israeli government. The team had to negotiate with these parties to gain access to the texts. This led to delays and complications in studying and publishing the scrolls.

**Limited resources:** The editorial team also faced limited resources, including funding, personnel, and technological support. This made it difficult for them to fully catalog and study all of the scrolls in a timely manner.

**Differences in scholarly approaches:** The editorial team was composed of scholars from different disciplines and with different approaches to studying the scrolls. This sometimes led to differences of opinion and conflicts within the team, which slowed progress and increased the challenge of reaching an agreement on matters related to interpreting the texts.

**Political and religious tensions:** The Dead Sea Scrolls were discovered in an area amid ongoing political and religious tensions, which sometimes made it difficult for the editorial team to work effectively and, at times, simply be onsite. The team faced criticism and pressure from various groups, including the Israeli government, the Catholic Church, and various Jewish organizations, making it challenging to focus on their scholarly work.

Although the editorial team of the Dead Sea Scrolls faced many challenges and delays in their efforts to study and publish the scrolls, they made significant progress in understanding and interpreting these important historical texts.[44]

## 5.3 Team Leadership

Roland de Vaux was a French archaeologist and Dominican priest best known for his role as the leader of the International Team. He was appointed head of the team in 1952 and held this position until his death in 1971.

As the team leader, de Vaux coordinated the efforts of the many scholars involved in the study and translation of the scrolls. He also played a significant role in the negotiation process, speaking with the various parties who owned or controlled the scrolls, including the Israeli government and various private collectors.

De Vaux's leadership of the editorial team was not without controversy, and he faced criticism from some quarters for his handling of the scrolls and his management of the team. Some scholars accused him of being too secretive and controlling in his approach, and there were also allegations that he was biased in favor of certain interpretations of the scrolls. Despite these controversies, de Vaux is widely acknowledged for contributing to establishing the groundwork for the ongoing study and understanding of the Dead Sea Scrolls.

Following Father de Vaux's death in 1971, there was a series of qualified, talented team leaders:

- Father Josef Milik, a Catholic scholar of Semitic languages, 1971 – 1984.
- Professor Emanuel Tov, a Jewish scholar of the Hebrew Bible, 1984 – 1990.

- Professor Elisha Qimron, a Jewish scholar of the Hebrew Bible, 1990 – 1998.
- Professor Sidnie White Crawford, an expert in Hebrew Bible and ancient Judaism, 1998 – 2002.
- Professor John Strugnell, a specialist in the Hebrew Bible and history of Judaism, 2002 – 2005.
- Professor Hanan Eshel, an expert in the Israel archaeology and history of Judaism, 2005 – 2013.
- Upon Eshel's death in 2013, Professor Adolfo D. Roitman, an expert in the study of the Hebrew Bible and ancient Judaism, took over the editorial team for the Dead Sea Scrolls. Dr Roitman is currently the Curator of the Dead Sea Scrolls and Head of the Shrine of the Book.

While the team has undergone several changes in leadership over the years, it has always been composed of scholars who are experts in the languages, cultures, and histories of ancient Judaism and are dedicated to studying and interpreting the scrolls.[45]

## 5.4 Criticism and Controversy

The Dead Sea Scrolls editorial team has faced considerable criticism and controversy over the years, particularly regarding its handling of the scrolls and the process of their publication and interpretation. Key criticisms include:

- **Lack of Transparency:** Scholars have accused the team of being overly secretive and restrictive, limiting access to the texts for independent study and analysis. This has fueled concerns that certain interpretations were unduly influenced by specific agendas, stifling open, collaborative scholarship.
- **Delays in Publication:** The slow pace at which the scrolls were published has also drawn criticism. These delays hindered the dissemination of information and slowed research progress, with some arguing that the team failed to make the scrolls accessible to scholars and the public.
- **Lack of Inclusivity:** The original team consisted of eight scholars, none of whom were Jewish, leading to accusations of bias. Critics argued that the team did not represent a full range of scholarly perspectives, which may have skewed interpretations of the scrolls.

In response to these criticisms, the editorial team has undergone significant changes. The team has been expanded to include scholars from a broader range of disciplines and backgrounds, enhancing inclusivity and representation. Efforts have also been made to improve transparency and accessibility, leading to a more open and collaborative approach to the study and interpretation of the scrolls.

## 5.5 Team Evolution and Expansion

Over the past few decades, the editorial team for the Dead Sea Scrolls has evolved significantly in response to earlier criticisms. The team has expanded to include a more diverse group of scholars, encompassing a broader range of disciplines and backgrounds. This evolution has facilitated a more inclusive and transparent approach to the study of the scrolls.

One of the most significant developments has been the incorporation of digital technologies and online resources, which have revolutionized the accessibility and analysis of the texts. These tools have made it easier for scholars worldwide to engage with the scrolls, promoting a more collaborative and transparent scholarship process.

Today, the editorial team is committed to fostering an open, inclusive, and technologically advanced approach to studying the Dead Sea Scrolls, ensuring that these ancient texts continue to inform and inspire scholarship across the globe.[46]

## 5.6 Freeing the Scrolls

The Dead Sea Scrolls were made widely available to scholars and the public in 1991 when the Huntington Library in California acquired a collection and made them available for unrestricted study through digital publication. Before this, scrolls' access was restricted to the small editorial team that faced criticism for its slow pace of publication and secretive approach.

The Huntington Library's acquisition of the scrolls marked a significant shift in the way they were studied and made available to the public, leading to a surge in research and analysis.

The digitization of the scrolls has made them more widely available and easier to access, with digital copies easily shared and accessible from anywhere with an internet connection. In addition, the digital publication has provided tools and resources that make it easier for scholars to access and analyze the texts, helping to further our understanding of these important historical documents.

The public availability and accessibility of the scrolls is likely the single most important event in helping to further our understanding of these important historical texts.[47]

## 5.7 Publication of the Scrolls

Many Dead Sea Scrolls have been published in a series of volumes known as the Discoveries in the Judaean Desert (DJD) series. Oxford University Press publishes the DJD series, which is edited by a team of scholars working at Oxford's Centre for Hebrew and Jewish Studies.

Thirty-eight volumes have been published in the Discoveries in the Judaean Desert (DJD) series thus far. The series was initiated in 1955, and new volumes have been added periodically over the years. Each volume in the series presents a critical edition of a specific group or category of Dead Sea Scrolls, accompanied by extensive notes and commentary. The collections encompass a broad array of writings, spanning fragments from all books of the Hebrew Bible (except for Esther) and additional texts outside of the biblical canon, shedding light on the beliefs and customs of the Jewish society responsible for the scrolls.

The DJD series is considered the definitive edition of the Dead Sea Scrolls, and the volumes are an important resource for scholars and researchers studying the scrolls and their historical and cultural context.

## 5.8 Institutions Central to the Scrolls

The Dead Sea Scrolls have been extensively examined and analyzed. A number of institutions and governmental agencies have preserved them. Some of the notable ones include:

**Rockefeller Foundation**: In the 1950s, the Rockefeller Foundation funded the initial research on the Dead Sea Scrolls. This support was instrumental in the early efforts to study and publish the scrolls, and it had a notable role in establishing the editorial team responsible for overseeing their publication. The Rockefeller Foundation's funding of the scrolls' research was part of a broader initiative to support the study of ancient texts and cultures.

**Rockefeller Museum:** The Rockefeller Museum, formerly known as the Palestine Archaeological Museum, is located in East Jerusalem and was established by the British Mandate authorities in the 1920s. At the time of discovery, the museum was the main repository for the scrolls and served as their study and preservation center.

**Hebrew University:** The Hebrew University of Jerusalem is a leading research university in Jerusalem, Israel.

Many scholars who have worked on the scrolls over the years have been affiliated with the university.

**American Schools of Oriental Research (ASOR):** ASOR is a professional organization that promotes the study of the ancient Near East, including the region's archaeology, history, and cultures. In the late 1940s and 1950s, ASOR played a significant role in advancing scroll scholarship through its publication of the Bulletin of the American Schools of Oriental Research (BASOR). In addition, ASOR has supported the development of online resources and tools for the study of the scrolls, such as databases and digital editions of the texts.

**École Biblique et Biblique et Archéologique Française de Jérusalem (EBAF):** The EBAF is a French biblical and archaeological institute that has played a significant role in the study of the scrolls, particularly in the areas of ancient languages and archaeology. The institute has contributed to the publication of numerous scrolls and fragments and is an important center for the study of the scrolls and the ancient Near East. The EBAF also hosts regular conferences and workshops on the scrolls and related topics and has a robust research program in these areas.

**Israel Antiquities Authority:** The Israel Antiquities Authority is the governmental organization tasked with safeguarding and maintaining Israel's cultural heritage, including the Dead Sea Scrolls. The authority oversees the collection, cataloging, and conservation of the scrolls and facilitates research and access to the texts.

**Jordan Museum**: The Jordan Museum in Amman, Jordan, is a national museum dedicated to preserving and exhibiting Jordan's cultural heritage. The museum has a collection of several scrolls, including the unique Copper Scroll. The museum has organized a variety of exhibitions and events related to the scrolls and has played a key role in promoting the study of these important historical texts in Jordan.

**Leon Levy Dead Sea Scrolls Digital Library**: This is an online platform that provides access to digital copies of the Dead Sea Scrolls and other related texts. The library is a collaborative project between the Israel Antiquities Authority (IAA) and the Leon Levy Foundation and was created to make the scrolls more widely available and accessible to scholars and the general public.

The library includes digital copies of the known Dead Sea Scrolls and many other related texts, such as manuscripts from the Cairo Genizah. The library is searchable and includes tools and resources for scroll study, including high-resolution images, transcriptions, translations, and scholarly annotations.

**Shrine of the Book**: The Shrine of the Book is part of the Israel Museum in Jerusalem and is dedicated to preserving and exhibiting the Dead Sea Scrolls. The museum was purpose-built to house and display the scrolls, and it has played a significant role in the preservation and study of these important historical texts.

The Shrine of the Book is home to a number of the Dead Sea Scrolls, including the Great Isaiah Scroll, which is the longest and best preserved of the scrolls. The museum also includes many other exhibits and displays related to the scrolls, such as manuscripts, artifacts, and other historical documents.

In addition to its role as a museum and cultural center, the Shrine of the Book is also a research institute. It has supported numerous scholarly and research projects related to the scrolls. The museum has a library and a research center, and it has supported the work of scholars and researchers in the study of the scrolls.

**Picture 10**

***The Shrine of the Book.*** Shaped like a ceramic scroll jar lid and built to house the Dead Sea Scrolls found at Qumran, it opened in April 1965 as part of the Israel Museum in Jerusalem. Public Domain.
©2022 Center for Israel Education.
https://commons.wikimedia.org/wiki/File:Israel_-_Jerusalem_-_Shrine_of_the_Book.jpg

To summarize, the Dead Sea Scrolls study has been made possible by the contributions of many institutions and entities. The organizations mentioned in this chapter are just some of those that have played a vital role in bringing the scrolls to the attention of the academic community, religious scholars, and the general public. The study of the scrolls is deeply indebted to these and many other institutions for their work advancing scrolls research, and we will continue to benefit from their contributions for years to come.

**Picture 11**

***Shrine of the Book Interior Displays***. The top of the center display represents the end of a scroll handle. Below it the Great Isaiah Scroll is displayed. ©2022 See the Holy Land. Public Domain.
https://www.seetheholyland.net/shrine/

## 5.9 Figures in the Scrolls' Journey

The discovery, reconstruction, and publication of the Dead Sea Scrolls involved many important figures and scholars. A select few of the key individuals who have played a role in these processes include (in alphabetical order by first name):

**Eleazar Sukenik:** Sukenik was an Israeli scholar of ancient Judaism and the Dead Sea Scrolls. He was the first collector to purchase the initial (three) scrolls. He was involved in the very first study of the scrolls and made important contributions to understanding them and the history and culture of ancient Judaism.

**John Trever:** Trever was an American biblical scholar and archaeologist. He was one of the first scholars to examine and photograph the scrolls after their discovery in 1947. He played a key role in the early investigation of the scrolls and their significance for the study of ancient Judaism and early Christianity.

**Khalil Eskander Shahin:** known as Kando, was a Palestinian antiquities dealer who was involved in the sale of the first seven Dead Sea Scrolls in the late 1940s. Kando played a role in acquiring and selling the scrolls to Eleazar Sukenik and the Syrian Orthodox Church. Kando also had possession and later sold the Temple Scroll in 1967.

**Metropolitan Samuel:** Mar Samuel was the Metropolitan (Archbishop) of the Syrian Orthodox Church of Antioch in Jerusalem during the mid-20th century. He acquired four of the initial Dead Sea Scrolls in the 1940s and subsequently sold them in the mid-1950s.

**Muhammed edh-Dhib (and cousins Jum'a Muhammed and Khalil Musa):** These three Bedouin shepherds discovered the first Dead Sea Scrolls in 1947 in a cave near the Dead Sea. They brought the scrolls to a local antiquities dealer, who facilitated their sale to two collectors.

**Roland de Vaux:** De Vaux was a French archaeologist and scholar who played a significant role in the study of the Dead Sea Scrolls. He was the director of the École Biblique, a biblical studies institute in Jerusalem. He was head of the International Team of Scholars from 1952 to 1971 and led the excavation of Khirbet Qumran from 1951 to 1956.

**Yigael Yadin:** Yadin was an Israeli archaeologist, military officer, and politician active in the mid-20th century. He is best known for his work on the Dead Sea Scrolls and for securing the purchase of four of the first seven scrolls. He played a significant role in the study and publication of the Dead Sea Scrolls.[48]

The Dead Sea Scrolls' study has been made possible by the efforts of many people, only a few of whom are mentioned here. From the Bedouins who first discovered the scrolls to the people who have preserved and studied them, the journey of the scrolls has been a wide-spanning endeavor. Numerous scholars and researchers have helped to bring the scrolls to the attention of the academic community, religious scholars, and the general public. The study of the scrolls is deeply indebted to these and many other individuals for their tireless work. Scrolls research will continue to benefit from their contributions for years to come.

A more comprehensive listing of important scroll figures is located in Appendix B.

**Picture 12**        **Picture 13**

(12) ***Muhammed edh-Dib, Jum'a Muhammed, and Khalil Eskander Shahin (Kando)***. The Bedouin scroll discoverers and the antiquities dealer. Photo by James Trever.
© Israel Museum, Jerusalem.
https://www.imj.org.il/en/exhibitions/faces-behind-scrolls-0
(13) ***Metropolitan Samuel*** (Mar Athanasius Yeshue Samuel), Archbishop of St. Mark's Monastery, purchased four of the initial seven scrolls discovered. Photo by Charlie Mnoog.
© Israel Museum, Jerusalem.
https://www.imj.org.il/en/exhibitions/faces-behind-scrolls-0

**Picture 14**     **Picture 15**

(14) *Yigael Yadin*, an Israeli military head of operations and Dr. Sukenik's son, orchestrated the purchase of the four remaining original scrolls from Metropolitan Samuel of St. Mark's Monastery. Courtesy of: Eddie Hirschbein, Bitmuna Collections.
© Israel Museum, Jerusalem.
https://www.imj.org.il/en/exhibitions/faces-behind-scrolls-0
(15) *Eleazar Sukenik*, a professor at the Hebrew University of Jerusalem, purchased the first three of the original seven scrolls discovered.
Public Domain.
https://www.timesofisrael.com/toi-asks-the-experts-what-are-the-most-important-finds-of-israeli-archaeology/

**Picture 16**              **Picture 17**

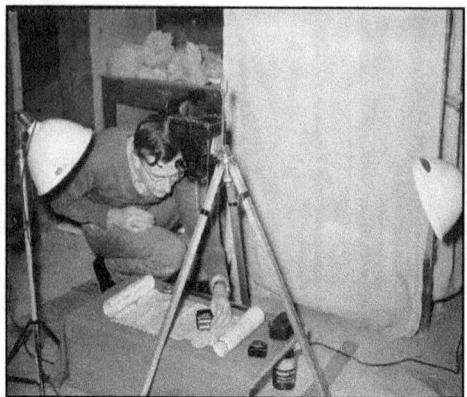 

(16) ***John Trever***, a biblical scholar and archeologist, was the first American to see the fragments and the first to photograph the scrolls. Photo by James Trever.
© Israel Museum, Jerusalem.
https://www.imj.org.il/en/exhibitions/faces-behind-scrolls-0
(17) ***Roland De Vaux***, École Biblique, was an early scrolls editorial chief and leader of the early 1950s Qumran archeological excavation. Courtesy of: Ecole biblique et archeologique.
© Israel Museum, Jerusalem.
https://www.imj.org.il/en/exhibitions/faces-behind-scrolls-0

# CHAPTER 6
# Ancient Sources

## 6.1 Ancient Religious Texts: The Big Three

Several primary ancient biblical texts have been used to evaluate and validate the Dead Sea Scrolls. These texts include the Masoretic Texts, the Septuagint, and the Samaritan Pentateuch.

**Masoretic Texts**: The Masoretic Texts are the traditional Hebrew texts of the Jewish Bible. They are named after the Masoretes, a group of Jewish scribes who lived in the 6th to 10th centuries CE and were responsible for producing and preserving these texts. The Masoretic Texts are the basis for most modern translations of the Hebrew Bible and are considered to be the most accurate and reliable versions of the text.

The Masoretic Texts are written in the Hebrew language and include the entire Hebrew Bible, including the Torah (the first five books of the Bible), the Nevi'im (the prophetic books), and the Ketuvim (the other writings). The Masoretic Texts are characterized by their careful attention to detail and use of a system of vocalization and accentuation marks that help preserve the text's pronunciation and meaning.

The Masoretic Texts are an important source for the study of the Hebrew Bible and have played a central role in the transmission and interpretation of the text over time. They have also been used as the basis for many modern translations of the Bible into other languages.[49]

**Septuagint**: The Septuagint is a Greek translation of the Hebrew Bible produced in the 3rd to 2nd centuries BCE. It is also known as the "LXX," a reference to the legend that it was translated by seventy (or seventy-two) Jewish scholars in Alexandria, Egypt. The Septuagint is an important text for the study of the Hebrew Bible and has played a significant role in the history of the Bible and its interpretation.

The Septuagint is written in Greek and includes not only the Hebrew Bible but also several additional texts not found in the Hebrew Bible, such as the books of Tobit, Judith, Wisdom of Solomon, and Sirach. The Septuagint is a valuable source for the study of the Hebrew Bible, as it provides access to an early translation of the text and helps shed light on its history and development.

Greek-speaking Jews and Christians widely used the Septuagint in the ancient world. It is still considered an important text for the study of the Bible and has been a source for many modern translations of the Bible into other languages, including English.[50]

**Samaritan Pentateuch**: The Samaritan Pentateuch is a version of the first five books of the Hebrew Bible used by the Samaritan community, a small group of Jews who lived in the Near East. The Samaritan Pentateuch is written in the Samaritan alphabet, a variant of the Hebrew alphabet, and is considered by the Samaritan community to be the authoritative version of the Torah. It includes some variations from the Masoretic Texts.

The Samaritan Pentateuch is an important source for the study of the Hebrew Bible. It provides access to an alternative version of the text and helps shed light on its history and development. The Samaritan Pentateuch has been used as a source for many modern translations of the Bible into other languages. It is often compared to the Masoretic Texts, the traditional Hebrew texts of the Jewish Bible, and other ancient versions of the Bible, such as the Septuagint.

These texts have been used to validate and interpret the Dead Sea Scrolls by comparing their texts to the Masoretic Texts, the Septuagint, and the Samaritan Pentateuch.[51]

## 6.2 Additional Ancient Manuscripts

Before the discovery of the Dead Sea Scrolls in 1947, the oldest surviving copies of the Hebrew Bible (also known as the Old Testament) were the Codex Vaticanus, the Codex Sinaiticus, and the Codex Alexandrinus. These three manuscripts are all Greek translations of the Hebrew Bible known as the Septuagint.

**Codex Vaticanus** is a Greek manuscript of the Old and New Testament, dating from the 4th century CE. It is named after the Vatican Library in Rome, where it is housed.

**Codex Sinaiticus** is a Greek manuscript of the Old and New Testament, dating from the 4th century CE. It is named after the Monastery of St. Catherine on Mount Sinai, where it was discovered in the 19th century. It is located within the premises of the British Library in London.

**Codex Alexandrinus** is a Greek manuscript of the Old Testament, the New Testament, and the Apocrypha, dating from the 5th century CE. It is named after the city of Alexandria, where it was likely written and is housed in the British Library in London.

It is important to note that all three of these manuscripts are incomplete, as they are missing some books or sections of the Bible. However, they are still highly valued for their textual accuracy and historical significance. They are among the oldest and most complete copies of the Bible that have survived to the present day.[52]

In addition to these ancient Greek translations, there also exists the **Latin Vulgate**, a Latin translation of the Bible that St. Jerome produced in the late 4th and early 5th centuries CE. The Latin Vulgate is significant because it was the official Bible of the Roman Catholic Church for many centuries and was the version of the Bible that was most widely read and studied in the Middle Ages. As a result, it has had a lasting influence on the development of the Western Church.

Like all translations, the Latin Vulgate is not a complete and literal copy of the original texts, but it is considered a faithful and accurate translation, still used by some scholars and liturgical communities today.

Next, several other primary extant manuscripts of the Hebrew Bible existed before the discovery of the Dead Sea Scrolls. These include:

**Aleppo Codex:** The Aleppo Codex is a medieval Hebrew Bible written in the 10th century CE. It is considered one of the most accurate and reliable copies of the Hebrew Bible and is often used as the basis for modern critical editions of the text.[53]

**Leningrad Codex:** The Leningrad Codex is a medieval Hebrew Bible written in the 10th or 11th century CE. It is the oldest complete copy of the Hebrew Bible in existence, and it is considered one of the text's most reliable manuscripts.[54]

**Cairo Genizah Manuscripts:** The Cairo Genizah manuscripts are a collection of more than 300,000 Jewish texts discovered in the 19th century in the genizah (storage room) of a synagogue in Cairo. The texts include many fragments of the Hebrew Bible and other Jewish writings from the medieval period.[55]

The Aleppo Codex, the Leningrad Codex, and the Cairo Genizah manuscripts all contain ancient content from the Hebrew Bible that dates near the time of the Masoretic Texts. Still, they are not considered to be Masoretic Texts.

Finally, in this section, we will discuss the Mishna, Talmud, and Targum, which have all influenced the interpretation and understanding of the Dead Sea Scrolls. These Jewish texts were written near the time of the Dead Sea Scrolls and contained similar themes and ideas.

**Mishna:** The Mishna is a collection of Jewish oral laws and traditions written in the 2nd century CE. It is the first part of the Talmud, a central Jewish text. The Mishna consists of 63 tractates, or books, that cover a wide range of subjects, including civil and criminal law, ethics, rituals, and ceremonies. It is written in Hebrew and is considered an important source of information about oral traditions and customs of the Jewish people in the early centuries of the Common Era.

**Talmud:** The Talmud is a collection of Jewish legal and ethical writings from the 5th century CE. It consists of the Mishna and the Gemara, a commentary on the Mishna. The Talmud is written in Hebrew and Aramaic and is considered one of the most important Jewish texts. It is a central text of Jewish law and tradition.

**Targum:** A Targum is a translation of the Hebrew Bible into the Aramaic language. Several different Targums, or Aramaic translations, of the Hebrew Bible were written between the 1st century BCE and the 5th century CE. The Targums are significant because they provide insight into how the Hebrew Bible was understood and interpreted by Jewish communities in the centuries after they were written.

The texts of the Dead Sea Scrolls have been compared to other ancient Jewish texts to understand their context and reconstruct the history and development of Jewish thought in the Second Temple period. In addition to the numerous texts mentioned, other ancient biblical texts were used to evaluate and validate the Dead Sea Scrolls. These included ancient copies of the Hebrew Bible written in other scripts and ancient translations of the Hebrew Bible into other languages, such as the Syriac and Coptic versions.

**Table 5**

| \multicolumn{2}{c}{**Ancient Literary Milestones**} ||
|---|---|
| 6th century BCE | Canonization of the Torah (Pentateuch), the first of three divisions of the Hebrew Bible |
| 4th century BCE | Canonization of the Nevi'im (the Prophets), second of three divisions of the Hebrew Bible |
| mid-3rd century BCE | Completion of the Septuagint (translation of the Pentateuch into Greek) |
| 200 BCE -100 CE | Apocrypha and apocalyptic literature |
| 40-50 CE | Beginnings of the New Testament |
| 90 CE | Canonization of the Ketuvim (the Writings), the third of three divisions of the Hebrew Bible |
| 200 CE | Mishna, first part of the Talmud (edits by Rabbi Judah) |

Source: Modified from the *"The Dead Sea Scrolls,"* Ellen Middlebrook Herron, ed. 2003.[56]

Scholars also used non-biblical texts from the same time, such as ancient Jewish writings from the Second Temple period, to help contextualize and interpret the Dead Sea Scrolls. These texts included the writings of ancient Jewish historians and writers and other Jewish writings from the same period. By comparing the texts of the Dead Sea Scrolls to these and other ancient texts, scholars could better understand the texts of the scrolls and identify any variations or differences between these texts and the traditional texts of the Hebrew Bible. These texts provide valuable context and insight into the interpretation and understanding of the Dead Sea Scrolls, as they represent different perspectives and traditions within Judaism.

## 6.3 Ancient Historians and Writings

The writings of ancient historians and writers such as Josephus, Pliny the Elder, and Philo of Alexandria have greatly aided the study of the Dead Sea Scrolls. These historic figures wrote about the period of the scrolls and specifically the Essene sect, providing valuable insights and information about this Jewish sect.

**Josephus** was a Jewish historian who wrote extensively about the Jewish people and their history. In his writings, he described the Essenes as a group of ascetic Jews who lived communal lives and adhered to strict laws of purity. He wrote about their belief in the resurrection of the dead and their opposition to the Sadducees.

Born Titus Flavius Josephus, he lived from 37 to 100 CE. His writings are an important source of information about Palestine's history and ancient civilizations. They offer an independent perspective on figures such as Pontius Pilate, Herod the Great, John the Baptist, James the Just, and possibly Jesus of Nazareth.[57]

**Pliny the Elder** was a Roman naturalist and historian who wrote about the Essenes in his work "*Natural History*." In this work, he described the Essenes as a group of Jewish ascetics who lived a communal life and practiced celibacy. He also wrote about their beliefs in the resurrection of the dead and their strict adherence to purity laws.

Pliny the Elder, whose birth name was Gaius Plinius Secundus, was a Roman author, scientist, and military leader who lived from 23 to 79 CE. He is known for his work "*Naturalis Historia*," an encyclopedia that served as a model for many later encyclopedias. In this work, Pliny mentions the Essenes, a group of people believed to have lived at Qumran, and places them west of the Dead Sea and north of Ein Gedi. This information supports the theory that the Essenes were the inhabitants of the Qumran plateau.

**Philo of Alexandria** was a Jewish philosopher who wrote about the Essenes in his works "*On the Contemplative Life*" and "*On the Virtues*." In these works, he described the Essenes as a model of piety and righteousness, known for their strict adherence to the laws of the Torah, their commitment to living simple, ascetic lifestyles, and their devotion to studying the Torah and other sacred texts.

Philo lived from 20 BCE to 50 CE. His deployment of allegory to harmonize Jewish scripture, mainly the Torah, with Greek philosophy was the first documented of its kind. He was one of the most prominent Jewish intellectuals of his time, and his writings have significantly influenced the development of Jewish thought in ancient and present times.

The writings of Josephus, Pliny the Elder, and Philo of Alexandria have provided immeasurable insights into the beliefs and practices of the Essene sect and the period in which they lived. These ancient historians and writers have contributed significantly to our understanding of the Dead Sea Scrolls and the Qumran community. Their works continue to be widely studied and discussed by scholars.

# PART THREE
# SCROLLS REVEALED

# CHAPTER 7
# The Scrolls Uncovered

## 7.1 An Overview

The Dead Sea Scrolls are diverse and include a wide range of texts that reflect the beliefs and practices of the community that produced them. This chapter will discuss three categories used to classify the scrolls, a note about the fragments, and a brief introduction to the first seven scrolls discovered.

**Biblical manuscripts**: The Dead Sea Scrolls include almost all of the texts that are part of the Hebrew Bible and additional texts related to the biblical canon. The texts of the Hebrew Bible represented in the Dead Sea Scrolls include fragments from every book of the Old Testament except Esther and additional texts such as the Apocrypha and the Pseudepigrapha. These texts are important sources for understanding the text of the Hebrew Bible and the way it was interpreted and understood in the Second Temple period.

**Non-biblical religious texts**: The Dead Sea Scrolls include numerous texts that reflect the community's religious and spiritual beliefs and practices but are not part of the Hebrew Bible. These texts include hymns, prayers, and other religious texts that provide insight into how the community worshiped and practiced its faith.

**Secular/community texts**: The Dead Sea Scrolls also include a number of texts related to secular life and the governance of the community. These texts include rules and regulations, historical texts, and other documents that concern the organization and functioning of the community.

The texts of the Dead Sea Scrolls offer valuable perspectives on the convictions and customs of the community that produced them. They are an important source of information for understanding the history, culture, and religious practice of the time.

## 7.2 Scroll Fragments Note

It is important to note that the number of fragmentary scrolls found in the Dead Sea Scrolls collection may be reported differently depending on the source, and these differences can be attributed to various factors. For example, some scrolls may be classified differently depending on how they were cataloged or due to ongoing debates about classifying very small or unreadable fragments. Additionally, some scroll fragments were discovered in caves outside the main Qumran area, and there may be disagreement about whether they should be considered part of the Dead Sea Scrolls collection.

Also, some scroll fragments from the Dead Sea Scrolls collection have included more than one book. In the case of the Torah, for example, it is common for the five books, or a subset of the five books (Genesis, Exodus, Leviticus, Numbers, and Deuteronomy), to be written together on a single scroll. This is known as a "Pentateuchal scroll," and such fragments were found among the Dead Sea Scrolls.

The Dead Sea Scrolls collection includes both complete copies of texts as well as fragmentary copies. In the case of fragmentary copies, it is often difficult to determine which text(s) are represented exactly, as the fragment may only preserve a small portion of the original document. In such cases, scholars may rely on various methods, such as paleographic analysis or comparisons with other known texts, to identify the text(s) represented by the fragment.

Note that *Fragmentary Scrolls, Texts, or Copies* refer to the number of individual, separate scrolls represented by many scroll fragments. For example, 50 fragments could have come from one scroll. Scroll *fragments*, on the other hand, are the number of individual pieces, not the number of scrolls they represent. Also, one scroll, consisting of multiple fragments, may contain more than one book.

## 7.3 The First Seven Scrolls

Seven scrolls were among the first Dead Sea Scrolls discovered and some of the most significant texts found. They have played a central role in the study of the Dead Sea Scrolls. These scrolls are briefly discussed below, and additional details about them are contained in chapters eight to ten.[58]

**Thanksgiving Hymns or Hodayot**: The Thanksgiving Hymns, also known as the Hodayot, are a collection of hymns and psalms written in Hebrew and dated from the 1st century BCE.

**Great Isaiah Scroll:** The Great Isaiah Scroll is a complete copy of the book of Isaiah, which is one of the prophetic books of the Hebrew Bible. It is written in Hebrew and dates from the 2nd century BCE.

**Isaiah**: The second copy of the Book of Isaiah, written in Hebrew, dates from the 1st century BCE.

**War Scroll:** The War Scroll is a text that describes a war between the "Sons of Light" and the "Sons of Darkness." It is written in Hebrew and dates from the 1st century BCE.

**Community Rule:** The Community Rule, also known as the Manual of Discipline, is a text that outlines the rules and regulations for members of the Qumran sect, the Jewish sectarian group that is believed to have produced and preserved many of the Dead Sea Scrolls. It is written in Hebrew and dates from the 1st century BCE.

**Genesis Apocryphon:** The Genesis Apocryphon is a text that expands upon the story of Lamech, a figure from the book of Genesis in the Hebrew Bible. It is written in Aramaic and dates from the 1st century BCE.

**Pesher on Habakkuk:** The Pesher on Habakkuk is a commentary on the book of Habakkuk, which is one of the prophetic books of the Hebrew Bible. It is written in Hebrew and dates from the 1st century BCE.

**Picture 18**

***The Great Isaiah Scroll*** (1QIsaa) is one of the original seven Dead Sea Scrolls discovered in Qumran in 1947. It is the largest (734 cm) and best preserved of all the biblical scrolls and the only one that is almost complete. Photo by David Harris,
© Israel Museum, Jerusalem. Public Domain.
https://www.mrm.org/dead-sea-scrolls

The Thanksgiving Hymns, Second Book of Isaiah, and War Scroll were among the initial group of scrolls purchased by Eleazar Sukenik, a professor of archaeology, from the antiquities dealer Kando.

The last four scrolls, the Community Rule, the Genesis Apocryphon, the Great Isaiah Scroll, and the Pesher on Habakkuk, were initially purchased by the Metropolitan Samuel, the head of the Syrian Orthodox Church in Jerusalem, and later procured by Sukenik's son, Yaegel Yadin, on behalf of the State of Israel.

These scrolls are among the most well-known and studied Dead Sea Scrolls. The first of these scrolls was published between 1947 and 1948, through a sequence of articles in the journal "The Bulletin of the American Schools of Oriental Research," and all seven were published by the early 1950s.

The first publication of the scrolls was coordinated by the Jordan Department of Antiquities and the Palestine Archaeological Museum (later the Rockefeller Museum). The publication process was slow and complex, and it was not until the 1990s that all of the scrolls were finally made available to the public.[59]

## Table 6

### First Seven Scrolls Discovered[60]

| Scroll Identifier | Scroll Name | Bible Association | Language | Date |
|---|---|---|---|---|
| 1QIsaa | Great Isaiah Scroll | Isaiah 1:1–31; 2:1–22; 3:1–5:30; 6:1–13; 7:1–25; 8:1–23; 9:1–20; 10:1–34; 11:1–45:25; 46:1–66:24 | Hebrew | late 2nd century BCE between 125 and 100 BCE |
| 1QIsab | Isaiah | The Book of Isaiah | Hebrew | 1st century BCE |
| 1QS | Community Rule (Serekh ha-Yahad) | | Hebrew | 1st century BCE |
| 1QpHab | Pesher on Habakkuk | Habakkuk 1-2 | Hebrew | latter half of the 1st century BCE |
| 1QM | War Scroll | | Hebrew | 1st century BCE |
| 1QH[a] | Thanksgiving Hymns or Hodayot | | Hebrew | 1st century BCE |
| 1QapGen | Genesis Apocryphon | Genesis 12:18–15:4 | Aramaic | 25 BCE–50 CE |

Source: "Dead Sea Scrolls," *Wikipedia*.
https://en.wikipedia.org/wiki/Dead_Sea_Scrolls

# CHAPTER 8
# Religious Manuscripts
## 8.1 Biblical Manuscripts

The Dead Sea Scrolls provided an enormous corpus of religious biblical manuscripts. These were terrific archeological and historical finds as they shed light upon and, in most instances, confirm the Hebrew Bible. There are 225 texts from the Bible contained within the Dead Sea Scroll documents, comprising about 22% of the total number of scrolls. When including deuterocanonical (meaning of or pertaining to a second cannon) books, the total number of biblical texts within the scrolls increases to 235. The biblical texts found in the Dead Sea Scrolls include:

- The **Five Books of Moses** (also known as the Torah and the Pentateuch): These include the books of Genesis, Exodus, Leviticus, Numbers, and Deuteronomy.
- The **Historical Books**: These include the books of Joshua, Judges, Ruth, 1 and 2 Samuel, 1 and 2 Kings, 1 and 2 Chronicles, Ezra, and Nehemiah (excluding Esther).
- The **Poetic Books**: These include the books of Psalms, Proverbs, Job, and the Song of Solomon.
- The **Prophetic Books**: These include the books of Isaiah, Jeremiah, Lamentations, Ezekiel, and Daniel.

- The **Twelve Minor Prophets**: These include the books of Hosea, Joel, Amos, Obadiah, Jonah, Micah, Nahum, Habakkuk, Zephaniah, Haggai, Zechariah, and Malachi.[61]

The Dead Sea Scrolls include fragments of nearly all of the books of the Hebrew Bible, including Genesis, Exodus, Leviticus, Numbers, Deuteronomy, Joshua, Judges, Ruth, 1 and 2 Samuel, 1 and 2 Kings, Ezra, Nehemiah, 1 and 2 Chronicles, Job, Psalms, Proverbs, Ecclesiastes, Song of Songs, Isaiah, Jeremiah, Lamentations, Ezekiel, and the Minor Prophets. Thirty-eight of the thirty-nine Old Testament books were found, all except Esther.

The fragments of these texts found among the Dead Sea Scrolls are generally similar to the traditional text of the Hebrew Bible as it is known today, but there are some differences between the two. These differences generally include variations in wording, spelling, punctuation, and the presence or absence of certain passages.

Table 7 provides a further breakdown of the Biblical manuscripts discovered. This chapter will explore several biblical books that may have provided meaningful information concerning the Hebrew Bible.

Table 7

| Book | Wiki[62] | DSS Complete Story[63] | DSS and the Bible[64] | Meaning of the DSS[65] | Other Sites*[66] |
|---|---|---|---|---|---|
| Psalms | 36 | 36 | 36 | 36 | 3 |
| Deuteronomy | 30 | 29 | 30 | 30 | 3 |
| Isaiah | 21 | 21 | 21 | 21 | 1 |
| Genesis | 20 | 15 | 20 | 20 | 4 |
| Exodus | 17 | 17 | 17 | 17 | 1 |
| Leviticus | 15 | 13 | 13 | 15 | 2 |
| Minor Prophets | 9 | 12 | 9 | 8 | 2 |
| Daniel | 8 | 8 | 8 | 8 | |
| Numbers | 10 | 8 | 7 | 8 | 3 |
| Jeremiah | 6 | 6 | 6 | 6 | |
| Ezekiel | 6 | 6 | 6 | 6 | |
| Ruth | 4 | 4 | 4 | 4 | |
| Samuel | 4 | 4 | 4 | 4 | |
| Job | 6 | 4 | 4 | 6 | |
| Song of Songs | 4 | 4 | 4 | 4 | |
| Lamentations | 4 | 4 | 4 | 4 | |
| Judges | 4 | 3 | 3 | 3 | |
| Kings | 4 | 3 | 3 | 3 | |
| Joshua | 2 | 2 | 2 | 2 | |
| Proverbs | 5 | 2 | 2 | 2 | |
| Ecclesiastes | 2 | 3 | 2 | 2 | |
| Ezra | | 1 | 1 | 1 | |
| Nehemiah | | 0 | 1 | 0 | |
| Chronicles | | 1 | 1 | 1 | |
| Esther | 0 | 0 | | 0 | |
| **TOTALS**\*\* | 217 | 206 | 208 | 211 | 19 |

\* Nineteen scrolls were discovered in caves other than the twelve Qumran caves. Endnotes in column headers reference the various sources, which have been modified and combined in this table.

\*\*Totals do not agree but are "as reported" by the named source. See "Scroll Fragment Note" in chapter seven.

### 8.1.1 Genesis - Deuteronomy

The Dead Sea Scrolls collection includes many copies of the Torah, or the first five books of the Hebrew Bible (Genesis, Exodus, Leviticus, Numbers, and Deuteronomy), also known as the Pentateuch. Many of the scrolls in the collection are copies of these texts. The collection includes complete copies of the Torah and fragmentary copies of individual books and passages.

There were nearly 100 fragmentary copies of the Torah: Genesis (20), Exodus (17), Leviticus (15), Numbers (10), and Deuteronomy (30).

The importance of the Torah to the Qumran sect is evidenced by the number of copies of the Torah found among the scrolls. The Torah was considered the most sacred text in Judaism and was foundational to the sect's beliefs and practices. The sect clearly saw the preservation and study of the Torah as central to their religious identity and mission.[67]

### 8.1.2 Samuel

The Dead Sea Scrolls contain four fragments of the Books of Samuel, but they are not complete texts. Nevertheless, the fragments are similar to the version of the books of Samuel that is included in the Hebrew Bible. There are a few minor differences in the text of the Dead Sea Scrolls fragments of the Books of Samuel, but these differences are somewhat insignificant and do not impact the broader meaning or message of the books.

The scrolls include fragments from both 1 and 2 Samuel, which are similar but not identical to the Masoretic Text. For example, some fragments of the Dead Sea Scrolls contain variant readings, additional or omitted passages, and different spellings or word order.

Overall, the fragments of the Books of Samuel are considered valuable historical witnesses to the text and are not considered significantly different from the version accepted as canonical today.[68]

### 8.1.3 Ezra / Nehemiah

The Book of Ezra and the Book of Nehemiah are two separate books of the Hebrew Bible that are considered part of the canon by Jewish and Christian communities. The books are grouped together as a single book in the Septuagint, the Greek translation. They are historical books that tell the story of the Jews' return from exile in Babylon and the rebuilding of the temple and the walls of Jerusalem, but they focus on different aspects of this story and are likely written by different authors.

In the Dead Sea Scrolls collection, fragments of the book of Ezra were found in Cave 4, and the book of Nehemiah was likely found (although some dispute this). This may be because the book of Nehemiah is relatively short, and the fragments discovered were too small to identify the book decisively. It should be noted, nonetheless, that the dispute exists over the discovery of Nehemiah fragments in the Dead Sea Scrolls.

The fragments of Ezra from the Dead Sea Scrolls are written in Hebrew and are generally similar to the Masoretic Text, the standard Hebrew text of the Hebrew Bible. These fragments demonstrate the text's stability over time.

It is possible that the Qumran sect did not consider the Book of Nehemiah as significant as the Book of Ezra, or it may have been excluded from the collection for other reasons. However, the possible absence of the Book of Nehemiah from the Dead Sea Scrolls does not affect its status as an important and authoritative text in Jewish and Christian communities. It is still widely studied and revered for its depiction of God's faithfulness and sovereignty and its portrayal of the importance of rebuilding and restoring the community of believers.[69]

### 8.1.4 Esther

The Book of Esther is a book in the Hebrew Bible that tells the story of Esther, a Jewish queen of the Persian Empire who saves her people from extermination by the court official Haman. It was not found in the Dead Sea Scrolls.

There are a few possible reasons for this. One possibility is that the Book of Esther was not widely accepted as part of the Hebrew scripture canon when the Dead Sea Scrolls were written. Another possibility is that the Book of Esther was not considered relevant to the religious practices or beliefs of the community. It is also possible that copies of the Book of Esther were simply unavailable or not preserved in the region where the Dead Sea Scrolls were discovered.

It is noteworthy that the Purim festival which commemorates the deliverance of the Jewish people from Haman, and is only mentioned in the Book of Esther, is not included in Qumran calendars. The exclusion of the festival of Purim in the Qumran calendars may suggest that the Qumran sect did not possess or recognize the Book of Esther as scriptural.

The absence of the Book of Esther from the Dead Sea Scrolls discoveries does not necessarily mean that it was not considered important or that it was not widely read in ancient Judaism.[70]

## 8.1.5 Psalms

The Book of Psalms is a Hebrew Bible book containing a collection of 150 hymns, prayers, and poems. It is considered one of the most widely studied and influential books of the Hebrew Bible. Its teachings and prayers have played a significant role in developing Jewish and Christian beliefs.

The Dead Sea Scrolls collection includes many incomplete copies of the Book of Psalms. Specifically, 36 fragmentary copies of the book have been identified in the collection, making it the most well-represented book in terms of the number of copies. These fragments represent various parts of the book, some of which are quite small, containing only a few lines of text.

The presence of so many copies of the Book of Psalms in the Dead Sea Scrolls collection suggests that the book was considered particularly important to the Qumran community. The Book of Psalms comprises numerous hymns and prayers that would have been of particular interest to the Qumranites looking for ways to connect with God and express their devotion to Him.[71]

## 8.1.6 Isaiah

The Book of Isaiah is a Hebrew Bible book that contains the prophet Isaiah's writings. He is considered one of the major prophets, and the book's teachings and prophecies have played a significant role in developing Jewish and Christian beliefs.

The Dead Sea Scrolls collection includes 21 fragmentary copies of the Book of Isaiah. While many fragments are quite small, representing various parts of the book, one in particular, the Great Isaiah Scroll, is nearly complete.

The **Great Isaiah Scroll**, also known as 1QIsaa, is a significant artifact discovered among the Dead Sea Scrolls in 1947. It is considered one of the most well-preserved and complete scrolls of the Book of Isaiah found at Qumran, although it does have some minor damage in certain sections. The scroll is written in Hebrew and is estimated to date back to around 125 BCE, making it the oldest known complete copy of the book of Isaiah. It is also noteworthy for its large size, measuring at 734 cm (24 feet) in length and between 25.3 to 27 cm in height (10 to 10.6 inches) with 54 columns of text. The scroll is composed of 17 sheets of parchment.[72]

**Picture 19**

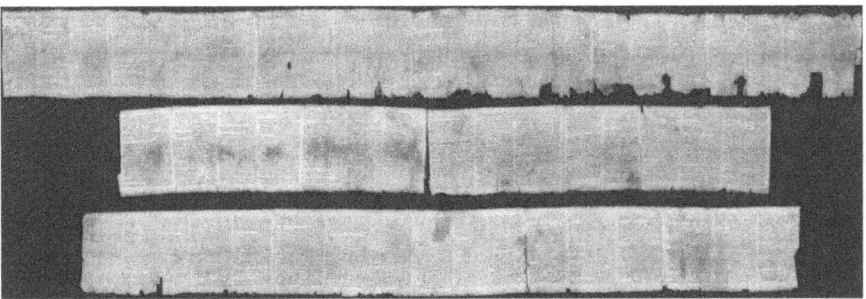

***The Great Isaiah Scroll*** (1QIsaa).
Photo by Ardon Bar Hama.
Public Domain.
https://en.wikipedia.org/wiki/Isaiah_Scroll#/media/File:Great_Isaiah_Scroll.jpg

The presence of so many copies of the Book of Isaiah in the Dead Sea Scrolls collection suggests that the book was considered particularly important to the Qumran community. The Book of Isaiah contains prophecies and teachings likely of interest to the Qumranites, who were looking for signs of the coming end times and the arrival of the Messiah.[73]

### 8.1.7 Daniel

The Book of Daniel discovered among the Dead Sea Scrolls is largely similar to the version of the Book of Daniel included in the Hebrew Bible. There are a few minor differences in the text of the Dead Sea Scrolls version of the Book of Daniel, but these differences are somewhat insignificant and do not impact the broader meaning or message of the book.

One difference between the Dead Sea Scrolls version of the Book of Daniel and the version widely accepted today is that the Dead Sea Scrolls version is written in Hebrew, while the accepted version is written in the form known as "Western Aramaic." There are also some differences in the wording and spelling of certain words and phrases and the order of the chapters in the two versions.

Overall, the Dead Sea Scrolls version of the Book of Daniel is considered a valuable historical witness to the book's text and is not considered significantly different from the version accepted as canonical today.[74]

In summary, the Dead Sea Scrolls collection contains a significant number of texts from the Hebrew Bible or Old Testament. These texts include fragments from every book of the Hebrew Bible except Esther. They are often used in conjunction with other ancient versions of the Hebrew Bible and other historical and archaeological evidence to understand better the context in which the texts were written and the perspectives of the people who wrote and transmitted them.

The scrolls are an important source for the study of the text of the Hebrew Bible because they provide evidence of the biblical texts as they existed in the Second Temple period before the canon of the Hebrew Bible was fixed. The Dead Sea Scrolls' biblical manuscripts provide insights into the history and development of the text of the Hebrew Bible and are an important resource for biblical scholars and historians.

## 8.2 Apocrypha, Pseudepigrapha & Deuterocanonical Books

The Apocrypha, Pseudepigrapha, and Deuterocanonical books found among the Dead Sea Scrolls are invaluable for understanding the development of the biblical canon and the religious beliefs and practices of the Jewish community during the Second Temple period. These texts not only provide insight into the diversity of literature circulated among Jewish communities in the ancient world but also illuminate the complex process of canonization within Judaism.

Before we dive into the specific categories and styles of these texts, it's helpful to define and explain the characteristics that determine each category:

**Apocrypha:** The Apocrypha refers to a collection of ancient Jewish writings not included in the canonical Hebrew Bible but found in some versions of the Christian Old Testament, particularly within Catholic and Eastern Orthodox traditions. The term "Apocrypha" means "hidden" or "secret," and these books, often written during the intertestamental period (the time between the Old and New Testaments), contain historical, moral, or devotional content. Some well-known examples include 1 Esdras, 2 Esdras, Tobit, Judith, Baruch, and the Wisdom of Solomon. While these texts are valued for their religious and historical insights, they are not universally accepted as Scripture, with their canonical status varying among different religious traditions. The

Apocrypha is generally determined by its exclusion from the Hebrew canon but inclusion in certain Christian Bibles.

**Pseudepigrapha:** The Pseudepigrapha is a collection of ancient Jewish writings falsely attributed to biblical figures, hence the term "Pseudepigrapha," meaning "false writings." Despite their pseudonymous authorship, these texts, including the Book of Enoch, the Book of Jubilees, and the Testament of Levi, were influential in Jewish thought and early Christian literature. The defining attributes of Pseudepigrapha include their false authorship claims, their production outside the official canon, and their thematic focus on apocalyptic visions, ethical teachings, and other religious concepts.

**Deuterocanonical:** The term "Deuterocanonical" means "second canon" and refers to books considered canonical by some Christian traditions, such as the Catholic and Eastern Orthodox Churches, but not included in the Hebrew Bible or the Protestant Old Testament. Examples include Tobit, Judith, the Wisdom of Sirach (Ecclesiasticus), and the Wisdom of Solomon. These books are distinguished by their acceptance in certain Christian traditions while being excluded from the Jewish canon and Protestant Bibles. They hold significant religious and theological value in the traditions that recognize them as canonical, reflecting a broader understanding of the biblical canon.

The apocryphal and pseudepigraphical texts found among the Dead Sea Scrolls, such as the Book of Enoch, the Book of Jubilees, and the Testament of Levi, are considered to be of historical and cultural interest but are not part of the biblical canon in many Jewish and Christian traditions. In contrast, the Deuterocanonical books, like Tobit, Judith, and the Wisdom of Sirach, are considered canonical by some Christian traditions but not by others. Their presence among the Dead Sea Scrolls attests to the fact that some Jews regarded them as religiously significant during the Second Temple period, even if they were not universally accepted as part of the biblical canon.

In summary, the Apocrypha, Pseudepigrapha, and Deuterocanonical books represent different categories of religious literature circulated among Jewish communities during the Second Temple period. Their presence among the Dead Sea Scrolls offers valuable insights into the diversity of religious thought and the complex process of canonization in ancient Judaism.

### 8.2.1 1 Enoch

1 Enoch, also called the Book of Watchers, is an ancient Jewish text not part of the Hebrew Bible canon. It is, however, included in the canon of the Ethiopian Orthodox Church, which considers it an important religious text.

Among the Dead Sea Scrolls, 25 fragmentary copies of 1 Enoch were discovered. Due to the number of incomplete copies found in the Dead Sea Scrolls, it was likely considered important by the Qumran sect. Therefore, it may have been seen as having important religious or historical significance. It may also be included in the canon due to its status as an ancient Jewish text, as the Ethiopian Orthodox Church is an Oriental Orthodox Church with roots in Judaism.[75]

## 8.2.2 Epistle of Jeremiah

The Epistle of Jeremiah is a text included as a separate book in some versions of the Bible, but it is commonly considered a part of the Book of Baruch in the Hebrew Bible. The Book of Baruch is a book of the Hebrew Bible that is part of the deuterocanonical books in the Catholic and Eastern Orthodox traditions. It is not part of the canon of the Hebrew Bible but is included in the Septuagint, the Greek translation of the Hebrew Bible.

The discovery of the Epistle of Jeremiah in the Dead Sea Scrolls confirms that some Jewish communities in the ancient world considered it an important text. However, it is not considered canon by many Jewish or Christian communities today.[76]

## 8.2.3 Jubilees

The Book of Jubilees, also known as the Little Genesis, is a Jewish pseudepigraphical work that retells the biblical story from the Book of Genesis. It was likely written in the 2nd century BCE and is not considered part of the Hebrew Bible canon. Twenty-one fragmentary copies were discovered among the Dead Sea Scrolls.

The Book of Jubilees was believed to be important to the Qumran sect based on the number of Jubilees contains a detailed chronological account of the world's history, from the universe's creation to the Israelites' arrival in the land of Canaan. It includes narratives about the patriarchs and matriarchs of the Bible and laws and commandments for the Israelites. The book also introduces the concept of the Jubilee, a year of release and forgiveness that occurs every fifty years; fragmentary copies were found, and it may have been considered canon by some Jewish or Christian communities. It was possibly seen as having important religious or historical significance. Although most Jewish and Christian communities do not consider the Book of Jubilees part of their respective canons, it is of historical, cultural, and scholarly interest.[77]

## 8.2.4 Maccabees

1 Maccabees, 2 Maccabees, 3 Maccabees, and 4 Maccabees are books of the Bible that are part of the deuterocanonical books in the Catholic and Eastern Orthodox traditions. While absent from the Hebrew Bible, they are featured in the Septuagint, the Greek translation of the Hebrew Bible.

1 Maccabees, 2 Maccabees, and 4 Maccabees were discovered in the Dead Sea Scrolls. The discovery of these books in the Dead Sea Scrolls confirms that they were considered important texts by some Jewish communities in the ancient world. However, they are not considered canon by most Jewish or Christian communities today. The book of 3 Maccabees was not discovered among the Dead Sea Scrolls.[78]

### 8.2.5 Psalms 151-155

Psalms 151-155 are a group of five psalms that are found among the Dead Sea Scrolls. These psalms are not found in the traditional version of the Hebrew Bible, but some may be considered part of the biblical canon by some Jewish and Christian traditions. They are collectively referred to as The Five Apocryphal Psalms of David.

**Psalm 151** is a prayer for wisdom and understanding. It is a short psalm attributed to David and describes his victory over Goliath. It is not found in the traditional version of the Hebrew Bible, but it can be found in certain versions of the Septuagint Greek Orthodox Bible and Latin Vulgate.

**Psalm 152** is a hymn to God's deliverance. It appears to have been written by David when he was dealing with losing a sheep from his flock due to attacks by a lion and a wolf. It is a short psalm with six verses and a non-rabbinical tone and is thought to have been composed in Israel during the Hellenistic period.

**Psalm 153** is a prayer for God's protection and guidance. It is also attributed to David and is a thanksgiving to God for delivering him from the lion and the wolf he had slain. It has the same date and provenance as Psalm 152.

**Psalm 154** is a hymn to God's power and might. It is a prayer attributed to King Hezekiah of Judah, who is said to have composed it when enemies surrounded him. The prayer is a plea for deliverance from danger, similar in theme to other prayers in the Hebrew Bible, such as Psalm 18 and Psalm 46. Based on the script, the text was likely written around the 1st century CE.

**Psalm 155** is a hymn of thanksgiving for God's blessings. It is also a Hebrew manuscript. It has a theme similar to Psalm 22, but its origin and date are not certain. The fragments of Psalm 155 found among the Dead Sea Scrolls are very fragmentary and do not give a clear idea of the entire psalm.

Except for Psalm 151, these Psalm texts do not readily appear in any version of the Bible, and there is no concrete record of them being known or referred to before their discovery among the Dead Sea Scrolls. Some research indicates that Psalms 153-155 survive only in Syriac; however, tracing their true provenance and substantiating their previous awareness has proved elusive.

These psalms are not found in the traditional version of the Hebrew Bible, and their authorship is not mentioned in the texts.[79]

## 8.2.6 Testament of Levi

The Testament of Levi is a pseudepigraphical text that is part of the Dead Sea Scrolls collection. It is believed to have been written by the Qumranites. This text is an account of Levi's life, one of Jacob's sons and the founder of the tribe of Levi in the Hebrew Bible. It is written as a testament in which Levi imparts his wisdom and teachings to his descendants before his death.

This text contains stories and teachings about the role of the tribe of Levi in the history of Israel. It emphasizes the priesthood's importance and the Levites' role as mediators between God and the people. It also contains teachings about the end of days, the role of the Messiah, and the importance of following the laws of God.[80]

## 8.2.7 Tobit

The Book of Tobit is considered part of the deuterocanonical books in the Catholic and Eastern Orthodox traditions. It's not regarded as part of the official Hebrew Bible canon but is included in the Septuagint.

Five fragments of The Book of Tobit were discovered in the Dead Sea Scrolls. This confirms that some Jewish communities in the ancient world considered it an important text. However, it is not considered canon by most Jewish or Christian communities today.[81]

## 8.2.8 Wisdom of Sirach (Ben Sirah)

The Wisdom of Sirach, also known as the Book of Sirach or simply Sirach, is a book considered part of the deuterocanonical books in the Catholic and Eastern Orthodox traditions. While not regarded as part of the Hebrew Bible canon, it is incorporated into the Septuagint.

Three fragmentary copies of The Wisdom of Sirach were discovered among the Dead Sea Scrolls. This confirms that some Jewish communities of the time considered it an important text.[82]

To conclude, the apocryphal, pseudepigraphical, and deuterocanonical books found among the Dead Sea Scrolls provide valuable insight into the diverse range of literature circulated among Jewish communities in the ancient world and the complex process of canonization that took place within Judaism. The presence of these texts in the Dead Sea Scrolls attests to the fact that some Jews considered them of religious significance in the Second Temple period, and they enrich our understanding and interpretation of the Bible and the biblical canon.

# CHAPTER 9
# Non-Biblical Religious Manuscripts

Discovered in the Dead Sea Scrolls are numerous non-biblical religious manuscripts that are not considered part of the biblical canon by Jewish and Christian traditions. Nevertheless, these texts, which include the Genesis Apocryphon, Thanksgiving Hymns, Pesher on Habakkuk, Temple Scroll, and Reworked Pentateuch, are of religious and cultural significance and can enrich our understanding and interpretation of the Bible. This chapter will examine these non-biblical religious manuscripts in more detail.

## 9.1 Genesis Apocryphon

The Genesis Apocryphon is a non-canonical, extra-biblical text that is one of the first seven texts discovered among the Dead Sea Scrolls. It is a pseudepigraphical text, meaning that it is attributed to a biblical figure (in this case, Abraham) but was not written by that person. The text is written in Hebrew and is believed to have been composed around 50 BCE to 25 CE.

This text retells the story of Genesis, from the world's creation to the death of Abraham. It includes additional stories and details not found in the traditional book of Genesis.

The manuscript expands upon the story of Lamech, a figure from the book of Genesis in the Hebrew Bible. In the Hebrew Bible, Lamech is a descendant of Cain and is known for his violent nature and boastful words. It adds additional details to the story of Lamech and describes his marriages and his children.

The Genesis Apocryphon was initially referred to as the "Lamech Scroll" because the text contains a reference to the biblical figure Lamech. Because the scroll was difficult to unroll, that was all that was visible and known for some time. It is not part of the biblical canon or an officially recognized scriptural text by any major Christian denomination. It is, however, considered to be of historical and cultural interest and has been studied by scholars interested in the history and literature of ancient Judaism.[83]

## 9.2 Thanksgiving Hymns or Hodayot

The Thanksgiving Hymns, also known as the Hodayot, are a collection of hymns and psalms among the first seven Dead Sea Scrolls found. The title "The Scroll" originates from the frequent repetition of the expression "I am grateful" found in numerous poems within it. They are written in Hebrew and date from the 1st century BCE.

The Thanksgiving Hymns are hymns and prayers that express gratitude and thanksgiving to God. The texts are written in a poetic and highly formalized style, and they include themes and motifs common in ancient Near Eastern literature, such as the themes of creation, redemption, and divine kingship. Themes also include salvation, devotion to God, and the end times.

These texts are important because they are one of the earliest examples of Jewish liturgical literature. The texts are among the oldest known Jewish prayers, and they provide insight into the development of Jewish liturgical traditions over time.[84]

## 9.3 Pesher on Habakkuk

The Pesher on Habakkuk is a text that was one of the first seven found among the Dead Sea Scrolls. It is written in Hebrew and dates from the 1st century CE.

The Habakkuk Pesher is a commentary on the book of Habakkuk, which is one of the prophetic books of the Hebrew Bible. It is one of several "pesher" texts found among the Dead Sea Scrolls, which are commentaries on biblical texts that interpret them in a specific way. The Pesher on Habakkuk interprets the book of Habakkuk in the context of the Qumran sect's beliefs and practices.

The text of the Pesher on Habakkuk is structured such that it corresponds to the structure of the book of Habakkuk. Each chapter of the book of Habakkuk is followed by a corresponding section of the Pesher that provides an interpretation of the chapter. The text includes additional stories and details not found in the traditional version of the book.

The Habakkuk Pesher is one of the earliest examples of a biblical text interpreted in a way that was different from the traditional understanding of the text.[85]

## 9.4 Temple Scroll

The Temple Scroll is written in Hebrew and dates from around the 1st century BCE or CE. The Temple Scroll was discovered in Cave 11 in 1956 but did not come into scholarly hands until 1967. As such, it was the last of the near-complete scrolls discovered to date. The scroll is a non-canonical, extra-biblical text and is one of the longest scrolls in the Dead Sea Scrolls collection.

The Temple Scroll contains various materials. This includes statutes and rules pertaining to the building and functioning of the Temple in Jerusalem and laws governing various aspects of Jewish life, such as ritual purity, property, and social relations. The text also includes descriptions of the ideal organization of the Temple and its precincts and contains prophecies and eschatological (end times) teachings. Some scholars believe that the Temple Scroll reflects the views of a particular group or sect within ancient Judaism, while others view it as a more general expression of Jewish thought and practice in the Second Temple period.

This scroll is an example of Jewish literature known as a "pseudepigrapha," which refers to texts attributed to a biblical figure (in this case, Moses) but were not written by that person. The Temple Scroll is not considered part of the biblical canon or an officially recognized scriptural text by any major Christian denomination. Still, it is considered of historical and cultural interest.[86]

## 9.5 Reworked Pentateuch

The Reworked Pentateuch is a reworking or revision of the first five books of the Hebrew Bible, known as the Pentateuch or Torah. It is written in Hebrew and dates from the 1st century BCE. These texts are thought to have been written by the Jewish scholars of the Qumran sectarian group.

The Reworked Pentateuch texts differ from the traditional version in several ways. First, they contain additional material not found in the traditional version, such as new laws and additional interpretations of existing laws. Second, they contain alternative versions of stories and events found in the traditional Pentateuch and often present them differently.

It is not clear why the authors of the Reworked Pentateuch texts felt the need to rework the traditional version of the Pentateuch. Some scholars believe that they were attempting to correct what they saw as errors or inconsistencies in the traditional version, while others think that they were trying to provide additional guidance and interpretation for their fellow sectarians. Regardless of the motivations behind the texts, they provide an interesting window into the thoughts and beliefs of the Qumran sect and offer another perspective on the interpretation of the Hebrew Bible.[87]

In summary, the non-biblical religious manuscripts found among the Dead Sea Scrolls are of historical and cultural significance and have been studied by scholars interested in the history and literature of ancient Judaism. Although not considered part of the biblical canon by Jewish and Christian traditions, these texts provide a window into the beliefs and practices of the ancient

Jews who wrote them and offer valuable perspectives on themes and events found in the Bible.

## 9.6 Additional Extracanonical Texts

Several additional non-biblical religious texts considered extracanonical and pseudepigraphical have been considered significant to the study of the Dead Sea Scrolls.

The **Book of Mysteries** is a pseudepigraphical text found in the Dead Sea Scrolls. It is a collection of secrets and mysteries believed to have been revealed to a person called "the Teacher of Righteousness." The text is cryptic and symbolic, and scholars still debate its exact purpose and significance.[88]

The **Book of Giants** is a pseudepigraphical text that retells the story of the Nephilim, a race of giants mentioned in the Bible. The text expands upon the story of the Nephilim and describes their interaction with humans and their role in the world's history.[89]

The **Florilegium and Testimonia** are fragmentary texts in the Dead Sea Scrolls and consist of quotes and passages from various biblical and non-biblical sources. The texts are written in Hebrew. They are believed to have been compiled by Jewish scholars interested in preserving and studying the traditions of their ancestors. The Florilegium and Testimonia include quotes from the Hebrew Bible and other Jewish texts, such as the apocryphal books and the writings of the Qumran community.[90]

The **Nahum Commentary** is a fragmentary text that is a commentary on the biblical book of Nahum, a prophetic book in the Hebrew Bible. The commentary provides insights into the interpretation of Nahum by Jewish scholars during the Second Temple period.[91]

These five texts can be classified as extracanonical (not part of the Hebrew Bible) or pseudepigraphical (attributed to a person who did not actually write the text). They help provide insight into the Second Temple period and an understanding of the development of Judaism and early Christianity.

# CHAPTER 10
# Secular and Community Manuscripts

Among the texts found in the scrolls are many secular and community manuscripts that offer an understanding of the everyday routines, faith, and customs of the ancient Jewish authors. These texts, which include the Halakhic Letter, the Community Rule, the Copper Scroll, the Damascus Document, and the War Scroll, are of historical and cultural significance and have been studied by scholars interested in ancient Judaism. This chapter will examine these secular and community manuscripts in more detail.

## 10.1 Halakhic Letter / 4QMMT

4QMMT, also known as the MMT (Miqsat Ma'ase Ha-Torah) Scroll and the "Halakhic Letter," is written in Hebrew and dates from the 1st century BCE. The scroll contains a letter that discusses issues of Jewish law and tradition.

Scholars of the Dead Sea Scrolls and ancient Judaism have studied the content of the Halakhic Letter, and it has provided insight into the beliefs and practices of the group that produced it. Some of the topics discussed in the letter include:

- The proper observance of the Sabbath and other Jewish festivals,

- The appropriate way to offer sacrifices and perform other rituals,
- The importance of keeping kosher and other dietary laws,
- The proper way to conduct business and handle money, and
- The importance of maintaining purity and avoiding contamination.

The letter also includes references to various biblical texts and discusses the interpretation and application of these texts to the group's practices.[92]

## 10.2 Community Rule (Manual of Discipline)

The Community Rule, also known as the Manual of Discipline, is written in Hebrew and dates from the 1st century BCE. It is a collection of regulations and instructions that outline the beliefs and practices of a Jewish sectarian group.

The Community Rule is divided into several sections, each addressing a different aspect of the group's life and beliefs. Some of the topics covered in the Community Rule include:

- The organization and leadership of the group,
- The expectations and responsibilities of group members,
- The group's views on purity and holiness,
- The group's beliefs about the end times and the coming of the Messiah, and

- The group's interpretation of the Hebrew Bible and its teachings.

The Community Rule also includes many blessings and curses associated with obedience or disobedience to the group's rules. The Community Rule text is an important source of information about the beliefs and practices of this Jewish sectarian group. It provides insight into the group's understanding of the Hebrew Bible and its teachings, as well as its views on purity, holiness, and end times.[93]

## 10.3 Copper Scroll

The Copper Scroll is unique because it is inscribed on copper rather than a typical writing material such as parchment or papyrus. The Copper Scroll, believed to date from the 1st Century CE, is written in Hebrew and lists 64 various locations where valuable objects, such as gold and silver, are said to be hidden. The locations are described in detail and include information on the type and quantity of the hidden objects.

Although discovered in 1952, the Copper Scroll was not deciphered and translated until 1955. The copper had proven impossible to unroll, so it was cut into pieces to make it readable. Interestingly, John Allegro, one of the members of the team of scholars who worked on the Dead Sea Scrolls, led a failed expedition in the late 1950s to locate the hidden treasures described in the Copper Scroll. Despite the efforts of Allegro and others, the treasures the scroll describes have yet to be (or have already been) found.

**Picture 20**

***Copper Scroll Display.*** Strips of the Copper Scroll at the Jordan Museum. This is the only known inscription on metal from the Dead Sea Scrolls, and it was carefully cut apart in strips to be able to read it. This scroll consisted of three sheets totaling 230 cm in length.
Photo by Osama Shukir Muhammed Amin FRCP. Public Domain.
https://en.wikipedia.org/wiki/Dead_Sea_Scrolls#/media/File:The_so-called_Copper_Dead_Sea_Scrolls_at_the_Jordan_Museum,_from_Qumran_Cave_3,_1st_century_CE.jpg

The Copper Scroll has been the subject of much speculation and has generated a great deal of interest among scholars and the general public. Some people believe that the treasures described in the scroll are purely mythical and do not actually exist, while others believe that the treasures are real but have yet to be found.

Despite the fascination with the Copper Scroll, it is important to note that there is still much that is not known about it. The genuine intent and significance remain enigmatic and may never be comprehensively grasped.[94]

## 10.4 Damascus Document

The Damascus Document, also known as the Cairo Damascus (CD) or the Zadokite Fragments, is a Jewish sectarian text. It was first discovered in 1896 in the genizah (a storage room for old texts) of the Ben Ezra Synagogue in Cairo, Egypt. Fragments of the Damascus Document were also found in the Dead Sea Scroll caves.

The Damascus Document contains rules and regulations for the group members, including instructions for how to live a righteous and holy life and rules for the organization and governance of the group. It also includes a history of the group, including their origins and beliefs about the end of days and the coming of the Messiah.

The document was written in Hebrew and consisted of two main parts: the "Community Rule" and the "Damascus Covenant." The "Community Rule" section describes the beliefs and practices of a Jewish sectarian group known as the Yahad, or "Community," who lived in the Land of Israel during the Second Temple period. The group followed a strict interpretation of Jewish law and believed in the imminent arrival of a Messiah.

The "Damascus Covenant" section describes the history and origins of the Yahad and includes a series of rules and regulations for the members of the Community. It also contains prophecies about the end of days and the establishment of a new kingdom under the rule of the Messiah.

It is worth noting that the Damascus Document is thought to be a composite text, meaning that it was likely compiled from multiple sources and redacted over time. As a result, the document may not have been originally composed as a single unified work but rather as a collection of texts that were later brought together.

The Damascus Document is an important source of information about the beliefs and practices of a Jewish sectarian group during this period. It is considered one of the most significant texts from the Dead Sea Scrolls collection, as it was also found in contemporary times in the Cairo synagogue genizah.[95]

## 10.5 War Scroll

The War Scroll, also known as the War of the Sons of Light against the Sons of Darkness, was found in the first cave discovered in the Dead Sea region. The scroll is written in Hebrew and is believed to date to the 1st century CE.

The War Scroll is a lengthy text that describes a future war between the "Sons of Light" and the "Sons of Darkness." The text describes the forces of the sons of light as the "army of God" and the forces of the sons of darkness as the "army of Belial" (the devil personified). Finally, the text describes the various battles that will take place between these two forces and the eventual victory of the Sons of Light.

The War Scroll has been the subject of much scholarly research and debate, with different interpretations of its meaning and significance. Some scholars have argued that the text reflects the beliefs and expectations of a particular group of Jews living in the 1st century CE, while others have argued that it reflects a more general Jewish eschatological tradition.[96]

In summary, the secular and community manuscripts found among the Dead Sea Scrolls offer insights into the daily lives, beliefs, and practices of the ancient Jews who wrote them. These manuscripts provide a glimpse into the social, political, and cultural contexts of the time and a unique window into the world in which the Bible was written.

# PART FOUR
# ISSUES, IMPLICATIONS, AND INSIGHTS

# CHAPTER 11
# Issues and Themes in the Scrolls

The Dead Sea Scrolls contain various manuscripts with themes, concepts, and issues consistent with those found in the Bible and are important to both Judaism and Christianity. They include documents containing themes such as the apocalypse and end of days, the use of a lunar and solar calendar, the importance of communal property and initiation, the dualistic concept of light and darkness, and the celebration of festivals. Themes also include the depiction of certain figures or characters, the existence of laws and legal practices, the concepts of marriage and celibacy, the belief in the existence of a messiah, and the importance of purity and living according to a certain way or path.

## 11.1 Apocalypse, Eschatological, End of Days

The concepts of apocalypse, eschatology, and the end of days are related to the belief in the ultimate destiny of the world and the events that will lead up to that destiny. These concepts are found in various religious traditions, including Judaism and Christianity, and were commonly discussed in the Dead Sea Scrolls.

The idea of apocalypse refers to the end of the world by a transformative event that will fundamentally alter the course of human history. The term comes from the Greek word "apokalypsis," which means "revealing" or "uncovering." In both the Dead Sea Scrolls and the Hebrew Bible, the apocalypse is often depicted as a time of great turmoil and destruction, when God will intervene in the world to bring about the end of the current age and the dawning of a new age of peace and righteousness.

In the Dead Sea Scrolls, eschatology is closely tied to the belief in the coming of a messiah who will deliver the Jewish people from their suffering and lead them into a new age of salvation. The scrolls contain numerous prophecies and descriptions of the events that will precede the apocalypse, which encompass conflicts, calamities, and the emergence of deceptive leaders.

In the Hebrew Bible, eschatology is also closely related to the apocalypse concept. It involves the belief in the time of reckoning when God will mete out punishment to the unrighteous and reward the righteous. The Hebrew Bible contains numerous prophecies and descriptions of the end of the world, including the defeat of the enemies of God's people and the establishment of a kingdom of peace and prosperity.

The end of days, or end times, refers to the time when the world will end and the events that will lead up to that end. In many religious traditions, the end of days is seen as a time of great upheaval and change, when the world is transformed and God's ultimate plan for humanity is realized.

In the Dead Sea Scrolls, these were seen as central to the beliefs of the Jewish community at Qumran. Many scrolls contain descriptions of the end of days and the events leading up to it.

They often depict a vision of a future in which the forces of good will ultimately triumph over the forces of evil.

These concepts are frequently discussed in the Hebrew Bible, particularly in the prophetic and apocalyptic books. The biblical prophets often spoke about the end of days and the events that would precede them. Many of their prophecies are believed to have been fulfilled in the events of history. In the New Testament, Jesus and the apostles also spoke about the end of days, and many Christian traditions continue to hold these beliefs.[97]

## 11.2 Calendar: Lunar and Solar

Among the Dead Sea Scrolls collection texts are two types of calendars: a lunar calendar and a solar calendar.

The solar calendar used by some Jewish sects during the Second Temple period, such as the Essenes and the Qumran community, was based on a year of 364 days, divided into 12 months of 30 days each, with an additional day inserted at the end of the third, sixth, ninth, and twelfth month every year. This type of solar calendar follows a consistent pattern from year to year and results in holidays and other events that are fixed to specific days in the calendar falling on the same day of the week each year.

In contrast, the lunar calendar is based on the moon's phases and consists of approximately 354 days in a year, divided into 12 months of 29 or 30 days. Because the lunar year is about ten days shorter than the solar year, it is necessary to periodically insert additional lunar months (called intercalary months) to keep the lunar calendar in sync with the solar calendar. This means that the number of days in a lunar year can vary from year to year, and holidays and other events that are fixed to specific days in the calendar will not necessarily fall on the same day of the week each year. The Hebrew Bible mentions the lunar calendar, and the ancient Israelites used it to mark the sacred festivals and feasts of the Jewish faith.

The Dead Sea Scrolls contain both types of calendars, lunar and solar. Some calendars described in the scrolls are based on the solar year, while others are based on the lunar year. The Temple Scroll, for example, describes a solar calendar based on a year of 364 days, while other Dead Sea Scrolls describe lunar calendars based on the moon's phases. These calendars provide insight into the timekeeping practices and beliefs of the Jewish sectarian groups that produced or used them during this time.

The presence of both lunar and solar calendars in the Dead Sea Scrolls suggests that the Qumran sect was interested in accurately calculating the dates of the Jewish festivals and feasts. The use of both calendars may also reflect the Qumran sect's attempt to reconcile the traditional lunar calendar with the more precise solar calendar to better align with biblical teachings.[98]

## 11.3 Communal Property and Initiation

The concept of communal property is a central theme in the Dead Sea Scrolls. The scrolls contain several texts discussing the importance of communal ownership and its role in the Qumran sect's religious and social practices.

According to the scrolls, the Qumran sect believed that all property should be held in common and that community members should share in the ownership and use of resources. This belief was based on the idea that individual ownership and the pursuit of wealth were corrupting influences that could lead to conflict and division within the community.

The scrolls describe several practices intended to promote the concept of communal property and prevent the accumulation of wealth by individual members. For example, the scrolls contain rules governing the distribution of food and other resources. They prescribe penalties for those violating these rules or hoarding resources for personal use.

Initiations were also an important aspect of the Qumran sect's religious practices, and the scrolls contain several texts that describe the process of initiation into the community. According to the scrolls, initiates were required to undergo a period of probation and training. During this time, they were expected to adhere to a strict code of conduct and demonstrate their commitment to the community's values and beliefs.[99]

Upon completion of their training, initiates were formally admitted into the community and took a vow of allegiance to the sect. The scrolls describe this vow as a binding commitment to the community and its way of life, and they suggest that those who broke their vow could be subject to severe punishment.

The concept of communal property and the importance of initiation were central to the religious and social practices of the

Qumran sect, as reflected in the Dead Sea Scrolls. These practices were intended to promote unity and cooperation within the community and ensure its members remained committed to its values and beliefs.

## 11.4 Dualism: Light and Darkness

Dualism, or the idea of two opposing forces or principles, is a concept that is present in both the Dead Sea Scrolls and the Hebrew Bible. In the Dead Sea Scrolls, dualism is often expressed in terms of the opposition between light and darkness. Many of the texts found in the Dead Sea Scrolls depict a cosmic struggle between the forces of light and the forces of darkness. They often describe the forces of light as being associated with goodness, righteousness, and truth, while the forces of darkness are associated with evil, wrongdoing, and deceit.

One example of dualism in the Dead Sea Scrolls is the "War of the Sons of Light against the Sons of Darkness," which describes a future conflict between the forces of good and evil. The text describes a final battle in which the Sons of Light, representing the forces of good, will triumph over the Sons of Darkness, representing the forces of evil. The text also describes the role of a future messiah in this final battle and the eventual establishment of a new age of peace and righteousness.

Dualism is also present in the Hebrew Bible, particularly in the prophetic literature. In the Hebrew Bible, dualism is often expressed in terms of the opposition between God and his enemies and depicts the struggle between good and evil in the world. For example, in the book of Isaiah, God is described as a light that will ultimately triumph over the forces of darkness and bring about a new age.

Ultimately, dualism, as conveyed in the Dead Sea Scrolls and the Hebrew Bible, is a concept used to depict the struggle between good and evil and the ultimate triumph of good over evil. It is an important concept in the beliefs and teachings of the Qumran sect, the ancient Israelites, and the Hebrew Bible.[100]

## 11.5 Festivals

Texts found in the Dead Sea Scrolls contain descriptions of various festivals and feasts observed by the ancient Israelites, including the Passover, the Feast of Weeks (Pentecost), and the Day of Atonement (Yom Kippur). Nearly all the festivals described in the scrolls closely match those in the Hebrew Bible, of which several are:

The **Passover** is a festival that celebrates the emancipation of the Israelites from bondage in Egypt and their escape through the Red Sea. The festival is described in the Hebrew Bible and is one of the most important festivals in the Jewish faith. The Passover is also mentioned in several texts found in the Dead Sea Scrolls, including the "Community Rule" and the "Temple Scroll," which describe the proper times for observing the festival and its associated rituals.

The **Feast of Weeks**, also known as Pentecost, is a festival that shines light on the presentation of the Torah to the Israelites at Mount Sinai. The Feast of Weeks is mentioned in the Hebrew Bible and in several texts found in the Dead Sea Scrolls.

The **Day of Atonement,** or **Yom Kippur,** is a day of fasting and repentance that Jews observe as a way of seeking forgiveness for sins committed during the previous year. The Day of Atonement is mentioned in the Hebrew Bible and several texts found in the scrolls, including the "Community Rule" and the "Temple Scroll."

The Dead Sea Scrolls contain references to various festivals mentioned in the Hebrew Bible, suggesting that the group held these festivals and adhered to the associated biblical traditions and practices. This aligns with the general understanding of the Qumran sect as a group of Jewish religious ascetics who sought to live a devout and holy life in accordance with the teachings of the Hebrew Bible. The presence of these festivals in the Dead Sea Scrolls suggests that the Qumran sect was closely aligned with biblical teachings and traditions.[101]

## 11.6 Figures (Characters) Depicted in the Scrolls

The figures described below are important figures mentioned in the Dead Sea Scrolls because they play significant roles in the religious beliefs and practices of the Qumran sect. These characters help to reflect the sect's views on a variety of subjects, including theology, eschatology, ethics, and community life.

The **Teacher of Righteousness** is a figure mentioned in several texts from the Dead Sea Scrolls. According to these texts, the Teacher of Righteousness was a religious leader believed to be appointed by God to instruct people in the ways of righteousness. He is portrayed as a wise and faithful leader who his enemies persecuted.

The **Wicked Priest** is another figure mentioned in the scrolls. This figure is portrayed as a corrupt and oppressive leader who persecuted the Qumran sect and opposed the teachings of the Teacher of Righteousness.

**Cursed One** is a figure mentioned in several scrolls as a person God condemned for wickedness and rebellion.

**Man of Lies, Lying Man, The Liar, and Sprouter of Lies** is a figure mentioned in several texts as a person who spreads falsehood and deception.

**Son of God** or **Son of Man** is a title used in the Dead Sea Scrolls to refer to a person believed to have a special relationship with God. This figure is depicted as a savior or messianic figure that comes to rescue the people from their enemies and establish God's kingdom on earth.

**Sons of Light** and **Sons of Darkness** are terms used in the Dead Sea Scrolls to refer to two opposing groups or forces. The Sons of Light are depicted as righteous followers of God, while the Sons of Darkness are portrayed as enemies of God and opponents of the Sons of Light.

**Lion of Wrath** is a figure mentioned in the scrolls as someone who will come to judge the wicked and punish the enemies of God.

**Anointed One**, or **Messiah**, is a title used in the Dead Sea Scrolls to refer to a person believed to be the savior or deliverer of the Jewish people. This figure is depicted as a hero who will come to rescue the people from their enemies and establish God's kingdom on earth.

These are just a few examples of the many figures and roles mentioned in the Dead Sea Scrolls, which help to provide insight into the religious and social world of ancient Judaism.[102][103]

## 11.7 Law, Legal, and Punishment

The law, legal, and punishment system described in the Dead Sea Scrolls reflect the beliefs and practices of the Qumran sect. According to the scrolls, the Qumran sect was a religious community organized by strict rules and regulations. The scrolls contain several texts describing the roles and responsibilities of different community members and the laws and punishments applied to them.

The scrolls describe a hierarchy of authority within the community, with the community leaders holding the highest position of power. These leaders were responsible for interpreting and enforcing the community's laws, and a group of scribes and other officials assisted them.

The scrolls contain numerous laws and regulations that govern the behavior of members of the community. These laws covered various topics, including religious practices, social relationships, and personal conduct. For example, the scrolls contain rules governing the distribution of food and other resources, and they prescribe penalties for those who violate these rules or hoard resources for personal use.

The scrolls also describe a system of punishment for those who broke the community's laws. These punishments could include fines, restitution, public reprimands, and more severe measures such as exile or expulsion from the community.

Overall, the law, legal, and punishment system described in the Dead Sea Scrolls reflects the Qumran sect's belief in maintaining order and discipline within the community. These laws and punishments were intended to ensure that community members lived according to the sect's values and beliefs and to protect the unity and cohesiveness of the community.[104]

## 11.8 Marriage and Celibacy

The Scrolls contain some texts describing marriage restrictions in the Qumran sect. One of the main restrictions described in the scrolls is the prohibition on marrying outsiders of the sect. The scrolls stress the importance of maintaining the purity and integrity of the community and warn against intermarriage with outsiders, who were considered spiritually unclean.

The scrolls also describe restrictions on marriage based on familial relationships. For example, the scrolls contain rules prohibiting marriage between close relatives, such as siblings or first cousins. One text that discusses restrictions on marriage is the Damascus Document, which prohibits marriage to outsiders and to close relatives, stating that "no man shall take as a wife a woman who is near of kin to him, nor a woman a man who is near of kin to her" (CD 4:20-21).[105]

The restrictions on marriage described in the Dead Sea Scrolls reflect the Qumran sect's belief in maintaining purity and holiness within the community. They were intended to ensure that community marriages were conducted according to the sect's values and beliefs.

Whether or not the Qumran community was celibate is a matter of debate among scholars. Some scholars argue that the community was celibate, while others claim it was not.

The idea of celibacy in the Qumran sect was first brought to light in the writings of ancient authors Josephus, Pliny, and Philo. According to these ancient sources, the Essenes believed that celibacy was a way to achieve a higher level of holiness and purity, enabling them to devote themselves fully to their religious practices and beliefs.

Celibacy in the Qumran community can also be traced to its presence and discussion in some texts. For example, the Community Rule states, "no man shall take a wife" (1QS 1:10) and that "no man among them shall beget children" (1QS 3:12). Some scholars interpret these passages as evidence that the Qumran community was celibate.[106]

However, some scholars point out that several Dead Sea Scroll texts contain marriage restrictions and that female remains were found in the cemetery, suggesting that at least some community members were likely married.

Ultimately, it appears that the evidence for celibacy is inconclusive and that the Qumran community may have consisted of both celibate and non-celibate members.[107]

## 11.9 Messiah / Two Messiahs

Some of the texts found in the Dead Sea Scrolls contain references to the concept of a messiah or a savior figure who will bring about the end of days and establish a new age of peace and righteousness.

According to the Hebrew Bible, the concept of the messiah is central to Jewish belief and is mentioned in many different contexts. The Hebrew Bible describes a future messiah who will descend from King David and establish an eternal kingdom of peace and prosperity. In some texts, the messiah is described as a political leader who will restore the kingdom of Israel and defeat its enemies. In other texts, the messiah is described as a spiritual leader who will bring about the end of the world as we know it and usher in a new age of righteousness.

Some of the texts found in the Dead Sea Scrolls contain references to the concept of two messiahs, one from the line of Aaron (the Aaronic Messiah) and one from the line of David (the Davidic Messiah). The texts describe the Aaronic Messiah as a priestly figure who will lead the people of Israel in the observance of the laws of the Torah. While the Davidic Messiah is described as a political leader who will restore the kingdom of Israel and defeat its enemies.

The concept of two messiahs is not in the Hebrew Bible, and it is not clear where this belief originated. However, the idea of two messiahs may have developed within the Qumran sect in an attempt to reconcile different biblical traditions and expectations about the role of the Messiah.[108]

## 11.10 Purity

Purity was of concern to the Qumran sect, and the scrolls contain numerous texts that discuss the importance of maintaining purity in daily life. The concept of purity was also important to other Jewish sects and movements of the time, including the Sadducees, Essenes, and Pharisees.

The concept of purity, as discussed in the Dead Sea Scrolls, is largely in alignment with the biblical teachings on the subject. The Hebrew Bible contains numerous laws and commandments related to purity, including laws governing clean and unclean foods, the proper handling of bodily fluids, and the proper disposal of waste. The texts in the Dead Sea Scrolls reflect these biblical teachings and provide important insights into how the Qumran sect and other Jewish groups of the Second Temple period understood and applied these laws in their daily lives.

Purity was an important factor in the Qumran sect's beliefs and practices and was closely aligned with biblical teachings on the subject.[109]

## 11.11 "The Way"

In the Dead Sea Scrolls, the term "The Way" is often used to refer to the path or way of life that God prescribes. The scrolls contain several texts discussing the importance of following "The Way" to attain righteousness and salvation.

"The Way" is described in several texts in the Dead Sea Scrolls, including the Damascus Document, the Community Rule, and the Thanksgiving Hymns. In these texts, "The Way" is presented as a set of rules and principles that lead the behavior and beliefs of those who follow it. The scrolls describe "The Way" as a path of obedience to God's laws and teachings, and they often emphasize the importance of living a righteous and holy life in accordance with these laws.

This concept is mentioned in several books in the Hebrew Bible, including the Book of Isaiah and the Book of Proverbs. In the Hebrew Bible, "The Way" refers to the path or way of life prescribed by God, which leads to righteousness and salvation.[110]

"The Way" is a central concept in the Dead Sea Scrolls and is closely related to the themes of righteousness and obedience to God's laws and teachings. It is also important in the Hebrew Bible, and it is often used to refer to the path or way of life that is prescribed by God.

In summary, the themes mentioned in this chapter provide insight into the religious and cultural context of the Second Temple period. The presence of these issues and themes in the Dead Sea Scrolls serves as evidence of the continuity of certain beliefs and practices across Jewish history and highlights the roots of both Judaism and Christianity in the Qumran sect.

# CHAPTER 12
# Implications and Insights from the Scrolls

The scrolls are the oldest surviving copies of the Hebrew Bible and offer insight into the goings of the Qumran community and the religious and cultural world of their time. In this chapter, we will review the implications and insights drawn from the scrolls regarding the concept of canon, the determination of authoritative texts, and the idea that certain non-canonized texts may have been considered scriptural. We will also look at the relationship of the scrolls to the Hebrew Bible and Old Testament, Jesus of Nazareth, and the New Testament.

## 12.1 Authoritative Books

The Dead Sea Scrolls provide evidence that the Hebrew Bible, or Tanakh, was considered authoritative by the Jewish community that produced and preserved these texts. The Tanakh consists of the Torah (the five books of Moses), the Nevi'im (the Prophets), and the Ketuvim (the Writings). These texts were considered to be divinely inspired and were the basis for Jewish religious beliefs and practices.

In addition to the Hebrew Bible, the Dead Sea Scrolls also include texts considered of religious or spiritual significance by the Jewish community that produced them. These include texts such as the Book of Enoch, the Book of Jubilees, and the

Testament of Levi, which are considered important for understanding Jewish beliefs and practices of the time.[111]

### 12.1.1 Determining Relative Importance

There are several factors that scholars have used to determine the importance or relevance of the scrolls to the Jewish sect that produced and preserved them.

**Quantity of fragmentary scrolls.** The sheer number of copies of a particular scroll found at Qumran could indicate its importance to the sect. For example, if many copies of a scroll were found, it might be inferred that it was considered important enough to be widely disseminated among the sect's members.

**Frequency of mention or citation in other texts.** If a particular text is frequently mentioned or cited in other texts found at Qumran, this could suggest that it was considered important or influential within the community.

**Pesher/Commentary written.** Some of the scrolls found at Qumran are classified as "pesher" texts, which are commentaries on various books of the Hebrew Bible. The referenced books could be seen as important to the Qumran sect since they warranted special commentary.

**Evidence of centrality to sectarian beliefs or practices.** A text containing teachings or beliefs central to the sect's ideology or providing instructions for sect-specific practices could suggest that it was considered particularly important to the sect.

**Historical and Theological significance**. Texts that have played a significant part in shaping the development of religious tradition or have been imperative in shaping the beliefs and practices of that community could suggest importance within that tradition.

It is worth noting that these criteria are not necessarily exhaustive and that the relative importance of a particular text may depend on the context in which it is considered. Additionally, concerning religious manuscripts, it is important to remember that the Qumranites likely did not have a single, uniform "canon" in the same way that modern religious traditions do.

## 12.1.2 Texts Possibly Considered Scriptural by the Qumranites

Lawrence H. Schiffman, a scholar of Judaism and the Dead Sea Scrolls, in his book "*The Meaning of the Dead Sea Scrolls: Their Significance for Understanding the Bible, Judaism, Jesus, and Christianity*," discusses certain texts that were likely considered as scripture by the Qumranites.

According to Schiffman, the Qumranites considered several texts as scripture based on nine criteria. The text was or included: 1) statements indicating scriptural status, 2) an appeal to prophecy, 3) claims of divine authority, 4) Davidic superscriptions, 5) translation to Greek or Aramaic, 6) pesharim and commentary, 7) quoted or alluded to as an authority, 8) preserved in higher quantities, 9) dependence of earlier books.[112]

Based on these criteria, Schiffman proposes that the Qumranites likely considered as scriptural the texts of the Temple

Scroll, Jubilees, the Reworked Pentateuch, 1 Enoch, and the Epistle of Jeremiah.[113]

The **Temple Scroll** is a long and complex text found among the Dead Sea Scrolls. It is a legal text that deals with various topics, including the construction and function of the temple in Jerusalem, the rules and regulations for the Jewish festivals, and the laws governing the conduct of the Jewish people.

The book of **Jubilees** is a pseudepigraphical text that tells the story of the history of the world from the creation to the time of Moses. It is believed written by the Qumranites and considered to be of divine origin and authoritative by the community.

The **Reworked Pentateuch** is a group of texts written in Hebrew that consist of reworked versions of the first five books of the Hebrew Bible (the Pentateuch). The Reworked Pentateuch texts contain many of the same stories and laws as the traditional version of the Pentateuch, but they also include additional material and interpretive comments added by the Jewish community at Qumran.

**1 Enoch** is a pseudepigraphical text considered of divine origin and believed to have been written by the Qumranites. It contains teachings, laws, and prophecies and is considered important to the community.

The **Epistle of Jeremiah** is a letter attributed to the prophet Jeremiah, and it contains warnings about the dangers of idolatry and the importance of following the laws of God. It is considered of divine origin and is believed to have been written by the Qumran sectarians.

Schiffman's list of texts that were likely considered as scripture by the Qumranites is not exhaustive, and other texts may also fit the criteria he outlines. However, the texts he discusses are the most commonly cited as possibly scriptural for the Qumranites.[114]

## 12.2 Canon

The biblical canon, or the collection of texts that are considered part of the Hebrew Bible, was likely in the process of being defined during the time of the Dead Sea Scrolls. The Hebrew Bible texts represented in the Dead Sea Scrolls include sections from every book of the Old Testament, except Esther, and additional texts such as the Apocrypha and the Pseudepigrapha.

When the Dead Sea Scrolls were written during the Second Temple period, Jewish scholars and leaders may not have settled on the exact texts to be included in the biblical canon. Canonization, or the formal recognition of certain texts as part of the Hebrew Bible, was not fully completed until the 2nd and 3rd centuries CE.

One of the interesting aspects of the Dead Sea Scrolls is that they include many different versions of biblical texts. These variations can include differences in wording, spelling, and even content. For example, some of the texts found in the Dead Sea Scrolls contain alternate readings or additions to the biblical text that are not found in the traditional Masoretic Text, which is the standard text of the Hebrew Bible.

While the specific books considered canon may have been fairly well established at the time, the wording and content of the texts appear to have been somewhat fluid and possibly still undetermined.[115]

## 12.3 Hebrew Bible / Old Testament

The collection of ancient texts known as the Dead Sea Scrolls provides invaluable insights into the text of the Hebrew Bible, also known as the Old Testament and the history of its transmission. One of the most significant findings of the Dead Sea Scrolls is their high degree of textual consistency with the Hebrew Bible. The scrolls contain fragments of almost every book of the Hebrew Bible, and these fragments are largely consistent with the Masoretic Text. This refers to the conventional Hebrew text of the Bible that is presently employed by Jewish communities. This consistency suggests that the text of the Hebrew Bible was transmitted accurately over the centuries.

The Dead Sea Scrolls also reveal a great deal about the beliefs and practices of the Jewish people during the Second Temple period. These texts include hymns, prayers, and philosophical writings, and they provide insight into the religious and cultural context of the Hebrew Bible.

## 12.3.1 Differences

There are some differences and discrepancies between the texts found in the Dead Sea Scrolls and the texts found in the Hebrew Bible. These differences could be attributed to several factors, including differences in translation, the transmission and preservation of the texts over time, and the beliefs and practices of the various Jewish groups that produced these texts.

One of the main differences between the Dead Sea Scrolls and the Hebrew Bible is that the scrolls contain many texts not found in the Bible. These texts include works such as the Damascus Document, Community Rule, and Thanksgiving Hymns, which hold a wealth of information about the beliefs and practices of the Qumran sect and other Jewish groups during that time.

There are also some differences in the wording and content of certain texts found in the Dead Sea Scrolls and the Hebrew Bible. These differences could be attributed to differences in translation and the way the texts were transmitted and preserved. While there are some differences between these two sources, they also contain many similarities.[116]

## 12.3.2 Similarities

Both sources contain texts that are considered sacred by Jews and Christians. The Dead Sea Scrolls include fragments of nearly every book of the Hebrew Bible and many other Jewish texts considered important by Jews and Christians.

The scrolls contain a wealth of information about the doctrines and rituals of the Qumran community, and the Hebrew Bible provides the same of the Jewish people during this period. Both are considered important sources of authority and inspiration by Jews and Christians.

It is good to note that the Dead Sea Scrolls and the Hebrew Bible are important sources of information about the Jewish people's history, beliefs, and practices in the Second Temple period. The scrolls serve to complement and enrich our understanding of the history and development of Judaism and Christianity.[117]

## 12.4 Jesus of Nazareth

Jesus lived in Palestine during the 1st century CE, the same time as the Qumran sect and the Dead Sea Scrolls. However, the Dead Sea Scrolls do not mention Jesus Christ by name or directly relate to his life and teachings.

While the Dead Sea Scrolls do not mention Jesus Christ directly, they provide valuable insights into the cultural and religious context in which he lived and taught. For example, the scrolls include texts that provide information about the beliefs and practices of the Jewish people in the Second Temple period. Additionally, the scrolls include texts that discuss the concept of a suffering and triumphant messiah, which may have influenced the development of Christian beliefs about Jesus within early Christianity.[118]

## 12.5 New Testament

The Dead Sea Scrolls do not immediately mention the New Testament or any of its books. The scrolls consist primarily of Jewish texts that predate the New Testament and are not directly related to it. The scrolls include fragments from nearly every book of the Hebrew Bible and many other Jewish texts from the Second Temple period. On the other hand, the New Testament is a collection of Christian texts written in the 1st century CE and later that contains accounts of the life and teachings of Jesus and the activities of the early Christian community.

The Dead Sea Scrolls, however, provide valuable information about the cultural and religious context in which the New Testament was written. The texts in the Dead Sea Scrolls have helped scholars better understand the New Testament's background and context. The collection provides additional information about biblical texts and their significance in the broader context of Jewish and early Christian literature.[119]

In summary, the Dead Sea Scrolls offer abundant insights into the doctrines and customs upheld by the Qumran community and the religious and cultural world of their time. While they do not directly mention or contain any New Testament books, they provide a solid basis for understanding the period immediately before their creation.

# Conclusion

## The Takeaways

As we bring this journey of studying and understanding the meaning and impact of the Dead Sea Scrolls to a close, it is important to highlight a few key takeaways that emerge from this research. These takeaways represent informed positions on issues that have, at one point or another, been debated or contested and may continue to be questioned today. Through careful analysis and consideration of the available evidence, this author can assert the following:

- *Qumran Sect was Essene:* The sectarian and community documents found at Qumran, which include texts such as the Community Rule and the War Scroll, provide valuable information about the beliefs and practices of the Qumran community. These include ideas about purity, eschatology, apocalypse, dualism, the Messiah, and community property, leading many scholars to conclude that the Qumran community was an Essene sect.
- *Scrolls Involved Multiple Sources and Scribes:* While the Qumran community likely produced many of the Dead Sea Scrolls, it is also probable that other Jewish groups or individuals outside Qumran contributed to the collection. The sheer number of scrolls and the wide range of topics suggest that multiple sources and scribes were involved in their creation.

- *Additional Texts Considered Scriptural:* Some texts in the Dead Sea Scrolls collection, which were not included in the Hebrew Bible, may have been considered scriptural by the Qumran community. However, not all Jewish groups considered these texts scriptural, and their inclusion in the Hebrew Bible was not universally accepted.
- *Scrolls are Pre-Canon:* The concept of a fixed set of inspired or divine scripture, or canon, is evident in the Dead Sea Scrolls. The Qumran community had a distinct set of scriptures they considered authoritative. However, the process of canonization, or the establishment of a fixed set of texts as sacred scripture, took place over a longer period and was not completed until after the time of the Dead Sea Scrolls.
- *Scrolls Do Not Materially Change the Hebrew Bible or Old Testament:* The Dead Sea Scrolls contain manuscripts and references to books that are not included in the Hebrew or Christian canon, such as the Book of Enoch. The inclusion of these texts as biblical canon was not widely accepted, and they are not considered official canon by most Christian denominations. Therefore, the content of the Dead Sea Scrolls does not materially change the integrity of the Hebrew Bible or Old Testament.

- ***Scrolls Do Not Challenge Judaism or Christianity:*** The Dead Sea Scrolls do not directly challenge Judaism or Christianity. However, they provide insight into the beliefs and practices of a Jewish community that existed around the time of Jesus. Moreover, some ideas expressed in the Dead Sea Scrolls may have influenced the development of Christianity or were later adopted by Christians.

- ***Christianity Came Later:*** Christianity did not exist before the time of Jesus, who lived in the 1st century CE. The Dead Sea Scrolls, most of which were written before the time of Jesus, do not reference Christianity as it had yet to evolve. Christ's influence was not recorded in the scrolls. However, some of the ideas and beliefs expressed in the Dead Sea Scrolls may have influenced Christianity and were later adopted by Christians.

- ***No Direct Connection to the New Testament or Jesus:*** The Dead Sea Scrolls have been of interest to scholars of Christianity, as they provide a glimpse into the religious and cultural milieu from which Christianity emerged. However, the scrolls do not directly reference Christianity or the New Testament. They do not provide direct evidence for the historical Jesus or the events described in the New Testament.

- ***Unprecedented Insights into Second Temple Judaism:*** The period when the Dead Sea Scrolls were produced was a time not well documented in the Bible. The Dead Sea Scrolls are vital for understanding the history and beliefs of the Jewish community at Qumran, providing insight into the religious and cultural context of the time and offering a window into the world of Second Temple Judaism up to the time of Jesus.

- *Important Light Shed on the Origins of Christianity:* The discovery and translation of the Dead Sea Scrolls have significantly expanded our knowledge of the religious and cultural world of the Second Temple period. The scrolls have provided new insights into the history and beliefs of Jewish communities in the region and have helped to shed light on the origins and development of Judaism and Christianity.
- *New Knowledge Continues to Amass:* The study of the Dead Sea Scrolls continues to be an active field of research; discoveries and interpretations are regularly made. As such, our understanding of the scrolls and their significance will likely continue evolving and advancing.

## The Big Takeaway: Link to Early Christianity

The Dead Sea Scrolls represent one of the most significant archaeological and textual discoveries of the 20th century. While they offer a treasure trove of insights into the diversity of Second Temple Judaism, their most profound contribution may be the light they shed on the origins and development of early Christianity.

### *A Bridge Between Two Testaments*

The Dead Sea Scrolls bridge the so-called "silent" intertestamental period, providing invaluable context for the religious, social, and political environment from which Christianity emerged. They reveal a Jewish world rich with messianic expectations, apocalyptic visions, and a variety of religious practices and beliefs that foreshadow those of the early Christians.

### *Shared Messianic and Eschatological Expectations*

The scrolls underscore a shared messianic hope and eschatological vision between the Qumran community and the early Christians. While the Dead Sea Scrolls contain references to messianic figures and the idea of a new covenant, these expectations are more diverse and complex than those found in the New Testament. The anticipation of messianic leaders and a new covenant in the Scrolls highlights the continuity and transformation of Jewish thought leading up to early Christian beliefs about Jesus as the Messiah.

### *Communal Practices and Ethical Codes*

The communal living, strict ethical standards, and purity laws of the Qumran community parallel the practices of the early Christian communities. These similarities suggest that early Christian communal life and moral teachings were influenced by existing Jewish sectarian practices, as detailed in the Dead Sea Scrolls. Understanding these parallels helps us appreciate the formative influences on early Christian community structure and ethical norms.

### *Scriptural Interpretation and Theological Innovations*

The methods of scriptural interpretation found in the Dead Sea Scrolls, particularly the pesher commentaries, illuminate the interpretive strategies adopted by early Christians. The scrolls' inclusion of non-canonical texts and innovative theological concepts shows a fluid and dynamic religious environment where new ideas could take root and flourish. This environment set the stage for the theological innovations that would become foundational to Christianity.

## The Legacy of the Dead Sea Scrolls

In essence, the Dead Sea Scrolls are not merely historical artifacts but pivotal documents that connect the dots between Jewish traditions and the birth of Christianity. They reveal a complex and interconnected religious landscape, demonstrating that early Christianity was deeply rooted in Jewish thought and practice while also transforming these elements in light of new beliefs about Jesus as the Messiah.

### *Implications for Historical and Religious Scholarship*

For scholars, the Dead Sea Scrolls provide a richer, more nuanced understanding of the period leading up to the emergence of Christianity. They challenge simplistic narratives of a clear-cut division between Judaism and Christianity and instead highlight a period of vibrant religious interplay and evolution.

For contemporary religious thought, recognizing the deep connections between the Dead Sea Scrolls and early Christianity can foster greater appreciation and understanding of the shared heritage between Judaism and Christianity. It underscores the continuity of religious ideas and the ways in which faith traditions build upon and transform inherited beliefs.

## Concluding Thought

Ultimately, the "big takeaway" from the Dead Sea Scrolls is their vital role in illuminating the Jewish roots of Christianity. These scrolls significantly affirm the accuracy of the Hebrew Bible's textual transmission, providing us with access to much older copies than previously known. This validation has been crucial for scholars, confirming the integrity and preservation of biblical texts through the ages.

But the Dead Sea Scrolls offer us much more than ancient manuscripts. Their non-biblical community documents open a window into the beliefs, practices, and hopes of the Qumran sect, serving as a fascinating prelude to early Christianity. They reveal a rich, interconnected religious world, showing how early Christianity emerged deeply rooted in Jewish tradition, yet transformed by new beliefs about Jesus as the Messiah.

By studying the Dead Sea Scrolls, we gain profound insights into the origins of Christianity and the enduring legacy of Second Temple Judaism. They allow us to glimpse the religious world that shaped the earliest Christians, emphasizing the importance of Jewish thought and practice in forming Christian identity. Recognizing the deep connections between the Dead Sea Scrolls and early Christianity fosters a greater appreciation for our shared heritage. It highlights how religious ideas evolve and adapt over time, bridging ancient traditions with new faiths.

The Dead Sea Scrolls are not just historical artifacts; they are a testament to the enduring and evolving nature of faith. They offer a bridge between our past and our present, illuminating the path of spiritual continuity and transformation. They remind us that the roots of our beliefs are intertwined in ways that deepen our understanding and appreciation of our shared spiritual journey. The scrolls underscore the powerful legacy of Second Temple Judaism, shaping the contours of Christianity and reminding us that our spiritual heritage is both ancient and ever-new, constantly unfolding in the light of historical discovery and personal reflection.

---

"It was a tremendously exciting experience, difficult to convey in words, to see the original scrolls and to study them, knowing that some of the Biblical manuscripts were copied only a few hundred years after their composition and that these very scrolls were read and studied by our forefathers in the period of the Second Temple. They constitute a vital link – long lost and now regained – to those ancient times so rich in civilized thought and the present day."

> Yigael Yadin, *The Message of the Dead Sea Scrolls*, 1957
> Israeli archaeologist and scholar (1917-1984)[120]

# Appendix A
## Glossary

**Aleppo Codex** - Earliest codex of the Hebrew Bible. Completed around 920 CE.[121]

**Apocrypha** - the body of literature from 250 BCE to 200 CE that is not canonized by either the Hebrew Bible, Old Testament, or the New Testament[122]

**Bar Kokhba Revolt** - or the 'Jewish Expedition' as the Romans named it, was a rebellion by the Jews of the Roman province of Judaea, led by Simon bar Kokhba, against the Roman Empire. Fought c. 132–135 CE, it was the last of three major Jewish–Roman wars. Some historians also refer to it as the Second Jewish Revolt.[123]

**BCE (*Before Common Era*)** - is a secular version of BC (before Christ). **CE (Common Era)** - is the secular equivalent of AD (anno Domini).[124]

**Canon** - standard text of the official list of books considered to be Holy Scripture.[125]

**Circumcise Circumcision** - a covenant between God and all Jewish males, a symbol of purity, the ritual act of removing a male child's or adult's foreskin. In the New Testament, Christians are urged to be "circumcised of the heart" by trusting in Jesus and his sacrifice on the cross.[126] [127]

**Codex** - a group of manuscript pages attached on one side to form a book.[128]

**Deuterocanonical** - religious books considered by the Roman Catholic Church and Eastern Orthodox Church to be canonical parts of the Christian Old Testament but not present in the Hebrew Bible.[129]

**DSS** - Dead Sea Scrolls.[130]

**Eschatology** - derived from two Greek words and involves the study of "end things," whether of the end of an individual life, the end of the age, the end of the world, or the nature of the Kingdom of God.[131]

**Extracanonical** - being outside a canon of books held to be sacred.[132]

**Florilegium** (plural **florilegia**) - In medieval Latin, it was a compilation of excerpts from other writings and is an offshoot of the commonplace tradition. The word is from the Latin *flops* (flower) and *leggero* (to gather): literally a gathering of flowers or collection of fine extracts from the body of a larger work. [133]

**Fragmentary Scrolls, Texts, Copies** - This is the number of individual, separate scrolls represented by a multitude of scroll fragments. For example, 50 fragments could have come from one scroll. **Scroll fragments** are the number of fragments, not the number of scrolls they represent.[134]

**Halakha**- Jewish law. The body of Jewish oral laws supplementing the scriptural law and forming the legal part of the Talmud.[135]

**Hasmonean** - relating to the Jewish dynasty established by the Maccabees; a member of the Hasmonean dynasty, which was a ruling dynasty of Judea and surrounding from c. 140 BCE to 37 BCE. Forces of the Roman Republic conquered the Hasmonean kingdom in 63 BCE; Herod the Great displaced the last reigning Hasmonean client-rulers in 37 BCE.[136]

**Hellenism** - of or relating to Greek history, culture, or art after Alexander the Great.[137]

**Hellenistic Period**- covers the time between the death of Alexander the Great in 323 BCE and the emergence of the Roman Empire in 31 BCE.[138]

**Intertestamental Period** (Protestant) or **Deuterocanonical Period** (Catholic and Eastern Orthodox) - the period between the events of the protocanonical books and the New Testament. Traditionally, it is considered to cover roughly four hundred years, spanning the ministry of Malachi (420 BCE) to the appearance of John the Baptist in the early 1st century CE. It is roughly contiguous with the Second Temple period (516 BCE-70 CE) and encompasses the age of Hellenistic Judaism.[139]

**Khirbet** - an archeological site, is the conjunctive form "ruin of" and is the first part of many place names in the Middle East.[140]

**Masoretes** - the scribe responsible for inserting the vowels and accents onto a Hebrew Bible text.[141]

**Masoretic Text (MT)** - monumental work begun around the 6th century CE and completed in the 10th by scholars at Talmudic academies in Babylonia and Palestine to reproduce, as far as possible, the original text of the Hebrew Old Testament.[142]

**Melchizedek** - "king of righteousness," was the king of Salem and priest of El Elyon (often translated as "most high God"). He is first mentioned in Genesis 14:18–20,[2] where he brings out bread and wine and then blesses Abram and El Elyon.[143]

**Mishna (Mishnah)** - In Hebrew, meaning "repeated study." The oldest authoritative postbiblical collection and codification of Jewish oral laws, systematically compiled by numerous scholars over about two centuries.[144]

**Paleo** - *involving or dealing with ancient forms or conditions.*[145]

**Pentateuch** - means "5 rolls" or "five cases" refers to the first five books of the Hebrew Bible, also called the Torah in Hebrew and the books/law of Moses. In Greek, *penta* means "five," and *teuch* means "books."[146]

**Pesher** - a distinctive sectarian kind of commentary. Method of interpretation of biblical books in which historical context is understood as speaking to the present.[147]

**Procurator** - a treasury officer in a province of the Roman Empire.[148]

**Pseudepigrapha/ Pseudepigraphical** - the body of literature that purports to be written at an earlier time, usually by a biblical figure such as Adam, Moses, or Enoch. These writings are ascribed to various biblical patriarchs and prophets but were composed within approximately 200 years of the birth of Jesus Christ. Pseudepigrapha are not included in any canon.[149]

**Rabbi** - Hebrew meaning "my master".[150]

**Samaritan Pentateuch (SP)** - text of the Torah written in the Samaritan script and used as sacred scripture by the Samaritans. It dates back to one of the ancient versions of the Hebrew Bible that existed during the Second Temple period and constituted the entire biblical canon in Samaritanism.[151]

**Sect** - a group of people with somewhat different religious beliefs (typically regarded as heretical) from those of a larger group to which they belong. A group that has separated from an established Church, a nonconformist Church.[152]

**Sectarian** (Adjective) - denoting or concerning a sect. (Noun) - a member of a sect.[153]

**Septuagint (LXX)** - Greek Old Testament. The Torah was completed by the Jewish people of Alexandria circa 250 BCE. The remaining books were completed in the 2nd century. The Septuagint has four sections: law, history, poetry, and prophets. The books of the Apocrypha were inserted at appropriate locations.[154]

**Tetragrammaton** - "YHWH," the four sacred consonants, is the Hebrew acronym for the name of the God worshiped by the Israelites. The name may be derived from a verb that means "to be," "to exist," "to cause to become," or "to come to pass." While there is no consensus about the structure and etymology of the name, the form "Yahweh" is now accepted almost universally.[155]

**Talmud** - the body of Jewish civil and ceremonial law and legend comprising the Mishnah and the Gemara. There are two versions of the Talmud: the Babylonian Talmud (which dates from the 5th century CE but includes earlier material) and the earlier Palestinian or Jerusalem Talmud.[156]

**Tanakh** - The Hebrew Bible is the canonical collection of Hebrew scriptures, including the Torah (instruction), the Nevi'im (prophets), and the Ketuvim (writings).[157]

**Targum** - an ancient Aramaic paraphrase or interpretation of the Hebrew Bible, of a type made from about the 1st century CE when Hebrew was declining as a spoken language.[158]

**Torah** - the first five books of the Hebrew Bible, namely the books of Genesis, Exodus, Leviticus, Numbers, and Deuteronomy, also called the Pentateuch. *Torah* is Hebrew for "instruction".[159]

**Wadi** - a shallow, usually sharply defined depression in a desert region. In most instances, it may refer to a dry riverbed that contains water only when heavy rain occurs.[160]

**Yahad** - Hebrew meaning "unity" or "union". In some of the Dead Sea Scrolls, it appears as a designation of the group, usually identified as the Qumran sect or community.[161]

# Appendix B
## Figures in the Scrolls' Journey

Some of the key individuals who have played a role in the discovery, reconstruction, interpretation, and publication of the Dead Sea Scrolls include (in alphabetical order by first name):

**Edmond Wilson**: Wilson was an American biblical scholar who was involved in the study and publication of the Dead Sea Scrolls. He was a member of the international team of scholars that worked on the translation and interpretation of the scrolls and played a key role in the publication of the scrolls by the Dead Sea Scrolls Publication Project.[162]

**Eleazar Sukenik**: Sukenik was an Israeli scholar of ancient Judaism and the Dead Sea Scrolls. Sukenik was the first collector to purchase the initial (three) scrolls. He was involved in the very first study of the scrolls, and he made important contributions to understanding the scrolls and the history and culture of ancient Judaism.[163]

**Emmanuel Tov**: Tov was a professor of the Bible at the Hebrew University and later served as the editor-in-chief of the Dead Sea Scrolls Publication Project, a joint venture between the Israel Antiquities Authority and the Hebrew University that was responsible for the publication of the scrolls. Tov was also a member of the international team of scholars who worked on the scrolls' translation, interpretation, and publication.[164]

**Frank Moore Cross**: Cross was an American scholar of ancient Judaism and the Dead Sea Scrolls. Cross was a member of the initial team of scholars who studied and published the scrolls. He was a leading expert on the scrolls and played a key role in their translation and interpretation.[165]

**Geza Vermes**: Vermes is a Hungarian-born British biblical scholar and specialist in the study of the Dead Sea Scrolls and ancient Judaism. He was a leading authority on the scrolls and played a key role in their translation and interpretation.[166]

**Hershel Shanks**: Shanks is an American lawyer and archaeologist who has been involved in the study and publication of the Dead Sea Scrolls. He is the founder and former editor of the magazine "Biblical Archaeology Review," and has written extensively about the scrolls and their significance for the study of ancient Judaism.[167]

**J.T. (Józef Tadeusz) Milik**: Milik was a Polish biblical scholar, archaeologist, and a member of the international team of scholars that worked on translating and interpreting the scrolls. He played a key role in the publication of the scrolls by the Dead Sea Scrolls Publication Project.[168]

**James C. VanderKam**: VanderKam is a biblical scholar and professor who has written extensively about the Dead Sea Scrolls and their significance for the study of ancient Judaism and early Christianity. He is a specialist in the study of the Hebrew Bible and ancient Judaism and has published numerous books and articles on these topics.[169]

**John Allegro**: John Allegro was a British scholar who was a member of the initial team of scholars who studied and published the Dead Sea Scrolls. Allegro is best known for his controversial theories about the scrolls (alleging Christianity originated in an Essene clandestine cult centered around the use of psychedelic mushrooms), which the scholarly community has resoundingly rejected.[170]

**John Strugnell**: Strugnell was an English biblical scholar and archaeologist and served as the chief editor of the Dead Sea Scrolls project. He was a member of the international team of scholars that worked on the translation and interpretation of the scrolls and played a key role in the publication of the scrolls by the Dead Sea Scrolls Publication Project.[171]

**John Trever**: Trever was an American biblical scholar and archaeologist. He was one of the first scholars to examine and photograph the scrolls after their discovery in 1947. He played a key role in the early investigation of the scrolls and their significance for the study of ancient Judaism and early Christianity.[172]

**Khalil Eskander Shahin**: known as Kando, was a Palestinian antiquities dealer who was involved in the sale of the first seven Dead Sea Scrolls in the late 1940s. Kando played a role in acquiring and selling the scrolls to Eleazar Sukenik and the Syrian Orthodox Church. Kando also had possession and later sold the Temple Scroll in 1967.[173]

**Lawrence H. Schiffman**: Schiffman is an American scholar of Jewish studies who has written extensively about the Dead Sea Scrolls and their role in the study of ancient Judaism. He is a professor of Hebrew and Judaic Studies at New York University and has served as the editor-in-chief of the Dead Sea Scrolls Publication Project.[174]

**Martin Abegg**: Abegg is a scholar of ancient Judaism and the Dead Sea Scrolls. Abegg has made important contributions to the study of the scrolls, developing computer programs that have helped reconstruct and decipher the scrolls.[175]

**Metropolitan Samuel**: Mar Samuel was the Metropolitan (Archbishop) of the Syrian Orthodox Church of Antioch in Jerusalem during the mid-20th century. He was involved in acquiring four of the initial Dead Sea Scrolls in the 1940s and their subsequent sale in the mid-1950s.[176]

**Michael Wise**: Wise is an American biblical scholar and archaeologist who has written extensively about the Dead Sea Scrolls. He has been involved in the study and publication of the scrolls and served as a member of the international team.[177]

**Muhammed edh-Dhib (and cousins Jum'a Muhammed and Khalil Musa)**: These three Bedouin shepherds discovered the first Dead Sea Scrolls in 1947 in a cave near the Dead Sea. They brought the scrolls to a local antiquities dealer, who then facilitated their sale to two collectors.[178]

**Norman Golb**: Golb is an American scholar of Jewish history and literature who has written extensively about the Dead Sea Scrolls. He is known for his controversial theories about the origin and ownership of the scrolls and has argued that they were produced by a variety of Jewish groups in the period rather than by a single sect as was once commonly believed.[179]

**Robert Eisenman**: Eisenman is an American biblical scholar and professor who has written extensively about the Dead Sea Scrolls. He is known for his controversial theories about the scrolls and their relationship to early Christianity and has argued that they contain evidence of a rival tradition to mainstream Judaism that the early church suppressed.[180]

**Roland de Vaux**: de Vaux was a French archaeologist and scholar who played a significant role in the study of the Dead Sea Scrolls. De Vaux was the director of the École Biblique, a biblical studies institute in Jerusalem. He was head of the International Team of Scholars from 1952 to 1971 and led the excavation of Khirbet Qumran from 1951 to 1956.[181]

**Yigael Yadin**: Yadin was an Israeli archaeologist, military officer, and politician active in the mid-20th century. He was the son of Eleazar Sukenik and was best known for his work on the Dead Sea Scrolls and for securing the purchase of four of the first seven scrolls. He played a significant role in the study and publication of the Dead Sea Scrolls.[182]

# Appendix C
# Notes

[1] Yadin, Yigael. *Message of the Scrolls.* New York: Simon & Schuster, Inc., 1957,
[2] Ibid.
[3] Barker, Kenneth L., ed. *The NIV Study Bible.* Grand Rapids: Zondervan, 2011, 1570-1578
[4] DeSalvo, John. *Dead Sea Scrolls: Their History and Myths Revealed.* New York: Fall River Press, 2014, 148
[5] Cross, Frank Moore. *Dead Sea Scrolls.* Washington D.C.: Biblical Archeological Society and Society of Biblical Literature, 2007, 34
[6] Ibid
[7] Charlesworth, James H. *Bible and the Dead Sea Scrolls: Volume One: Scripture and the Scrolls.* Waco: Baylor University Press, 2006, 286-287.
[8] "Roman Conquest." *Wikipedia.* Last modified October 29, 2022. https://en.wikipedia.org/wiki/Perea.
[9] Golb, Norman. *Who Wrote the Dead Sea Scrolls? The Search for the Secret of Qumran.* New York: Scribner, 1995, 361
[10] Ibid
[11] Herron, Ellen Middlebrook, ed. *The Dead Sea Scrolls.* Grand Rapids: The Public Museum of Grand Rapids and Wm B. Eerdmans Publishing Company, 2003, 16
[12] "Bar Kokhba Revolt." *Wikipedia.* Last modified December 10, 2022. https://en.wikipedia.org/wiki/Bar_Kokhba_revolt.
[13] VanderKam, James C., and Peter Flint. *Meaning of The Dead Sea Scrolls: Their Significance for Understanding the Bible, Judaism, Jesus, and Christianity.* New York: HarperCollins Publishers Inc., 2002, 240-249.
[14] Ibid., 250, 280-282.
[15] Ibid., 252, 276.
[16] Pfeiffer, Charles F. *Dead Sea Scrolls and the Bible.* Grand Rapids: Baker Book House, 1969, 41

[17] Shanks, Hershel. *Mystery and Meaning of the Dead Sea Scrolls.* New York: Random House, 1998, 111-115, 125.
[18] Schiffman, Lawrence H. *Reclaiming the Dead Sea Scrolls: Their True Meaning for Judaism and Christianity.* New York: Doubleday Religious Publishing Group, Inc., 1995, xvii.
[19] "Qumran." *Wikipedia.* Last modified October 29, 2022. https://en.wikipedia.org/wiki/Qumran.
[20] Herron, ed., *Dead Sea Scrolls,* 16.
[21] Ibid.
[22] Ibid.
[23] Davies, Philip R., George J. Brooke, and Phillip R. Callaway. *Complete World of the Dead Sea Scrolls.* New York: Thames & Hudson Ltd., 2002, 168.
[24] Ibid.
[25] Allegro, John. *Mystery of the Dead Sea Scrolls Revealed.* New York: Gramercy Publishing Company, 1981, 93.
[26] Davies, Philip R., George J. Brooke, and Phillip R. Callaway. *Complete World.* 168.
[27] "Qumran Caves." *Bible Places.* Last modified July 30, 2022. https://www.bibleplaces.com/qumrancaves.
[28] Ibid.
[29] Ibid.
[30] Ibid.
[31] Ibid.
[32] Ibid.
[33] Ibid.
[34] "Qumran Cave 12: New Dead Sea Scrolls Cave Discovered." *SciNews.* Accessed November 10, 2022. www.sci.news/archaeology/qumran-cave-12-dead-sea-scrolls-04607.html.
[35] VanderKam, James C. *Dead Sea Scrolls Today.* Grand Rapids: Wm B. Eerdmans Publishing Company, 1994, 5-6.
[36] Ibid.
[37] Schiffman, Lawrence H. *Reclaiming the Scrolls.* 33.
[38] Ibid., 58-67.
[39] Ibid.
[40] Ibid.

⁴¹ Ibid.
⁴² "The Dead Sea Scrolls: 9 Common Questions, Answered." *Logos.* Accessed September 2, 2022. https://www.logos.com/grow/hall-dead-sea-scrolls.
⁴³ Davies, Philip R., George J. Brooke, and Phillip R. Callaway. *Complete World of the Dead Sea Scrolls.* 22, 30-33.
⁴⁴ Ibid., 23-27.
⁴⁵ "Cast of Characters." *Biblical Archeological Society.* Accessed August 22, 2022. https://www.biblicalarchaeology.org/daily/biblical-artifacts/dead-sea-scrolls/cast-of-characters.
⁴⁶ "Dead Sea Scrolls 75th Anniversary." *Bible Study Magazine,* 2022, 23-26.
⁴⁷ "The Dead Sea Scrolls are opened to the public." *College & Research Libraries News.* Accessed July 5, 2022. https://crln.acrl.org/index.php/crlnews/article/view/19723/23353.
⁴⁸ Ibid.
⁴⁹ Abegg, Martin Jr., Peter Flint, and Eugene Ulrich. *Dead Sea Scrolls: The Oldest Known Bible Translated for the First Time into English.* New York: HarperCollins, 1990, x.
⁵⁰ Ibid., xi.
⁵¹ Ibid., xiv.
⁵² Shanks, Hershel. *Mystery and Meaning.* 146-148.
⁵³ Ibid.
⁵⁴ Ibid.
⁵⁵ Ibid.
⁵⁶ Herron, ed., *Dead Sea Scrolls,* 16.
⁵⁷ Abegg, Martin Jr., Peter Flint, and Eugene Ulrich. *Bible Translated.* x.
⁵⁸ Shanks, Hershel. *Understanding the Dead Sea Scrolls: A Reader from the Biblical Archaeology Review.* New York: Random House, 1992, 79-99.
⁵⁹ Ibid.
⁶⁰ "Dead Sea Scrolls." *Wikipedia.* Last modified November 21, 2022. https://en.wikipedia.org/wiki/Dead_Sea_Scrolls.
⁶¹ Shanks, Hershel. *Understanding the Dead Sea Scrolls.* 79-99.
⁶² Ibid.

[63] Campbell, Jonathan G. *Dead Sea Scrolls: The Complete Story.* Berkeley: Ulysses Press, 1998.
[64] VanderKam, James C. *Dead Sea Scrolls and the Bible.* Grand Rapids: Wm B. Eerdmans Publishing Company, 2012, 3.
[65] VanderKam, James C., and Peter Flint. *Meaning of the DSS,* 148-149.
[66] "Dead Sea Scrolls." *Wikipedia.* Last modified December 24, 2022. https://en.wikipedia.org/wiki/Dead_Sea_Scrolls.
[67] Ibid., 104-111.
[68] Ibid., 115.
[69] Ibid., 118.
[70] VanderKam, James C. *Dead Sea Scrolls Today.* 61, 149.
[71] VanderKam, James C., and Peter Flint. *Meaning of the Dead Sea Scrolls.* 120, 189, 193.
[72] "Isaiah Scroll." *Wikipedia.* Last modified November 20, 2022. https://en.wikipedia.org/wiki/Isaiah_Scroll.
[73] Charlesworth, James H. *Bible and the Dead Sea Scrolls.* 80, 273.
[74] VanderKam, James C., and Peter Flint. *Meaning of the Dead Sea Scrolls.* 109, 129.
[75] Ibid., 194, 256, 299.
[76] Ibid., 185, 203.
[77] Ibid., 196, 258, 300.
[78] VanderKam, James C. *Dead Sea Scrolls Today.* 144.
[79] VanderKam, James C., and Peter Flint. *Meaning of the Dead Sea Scrolls.* 80, 273.
[80] "Levi, Testament of." *Encyclopedia.com.* Accessed December 1, 2022. www.encyclopedia.com/religion.
[81] VanderKam, James C., and Peter Flint. *Meaning of the Dead Sea Scrolls.* 163, 203-204.
[82] Ibid., 162, 185.
[83] Charlesworth, James H. *Bible and the Dead Sea Scrolls.* 183, 203, 227-230.
[84] Ibid., 235.
[85] Yadin, Yigael. *Message of the Scrolls.* 90.

[86] Shanks, Hershel. *Understanding the Dead Sea Scrolls*. 136, 143, 257, 377.
[87] Charlesworth, James H. *Bible and the Dead Sea Scrolls*. 210.
[88] Schiffman, Lawrence H. *Reclaiming the Scrolls*. 206.
[89] VanderKam, James C. *Dead Sea Scrolls and the Bible*. 81.
[90] Schiffman, Lawrence H. *Reclaiming the Scrolls*. 230, 235.
[91] Herron, ed., *Dead Sea Scrolls,* 78.
[92] Ibid., 212.
[93] Ibid., 217-219.
[94] Ibid., 238.
[95] Ibid., 202, 215.
[96] Ibid., 219.
[97] VanderKam, James C., and Peter Flint. *Meaning of the Dead Sea Scrolls*. 232, 257, 264, 363.
[98] Wilson, Edmund. *Dead Sea Scrolls, 1947-1969*. New York: Oxford University Press, 1969, 27, 70.
[99] Shanks, Hershel. *Understanding the Dead Sea Scrolls*. 193.
[100] Ibid., 163.
[101] Schiffman, Lawrence H. *Reclaiming the Scrolls*. 302-308.
[102] Ibid., 117-119, 232-238, 341.
[103] Yadin, Yigael. *Message of the Scrolls*. 92-98, 103-117, 169-170.
[104] VanderKam, James C. *Dead Sea Scrolls and the Bible*. 133-137, 163.
[105] Wise, Michael, Martin Abegg Jr., and Edward Cook. *The Dead Sea Scrolls: A New Translation*. New York: HarperSanFrancisco, 1996.
[106] Ibid.
[107] Schiffman, Lawrence H. *Reclaiming the Scrolls*. 122.
[108] VanderKam, James C., and Peter Flint. *Meaning of the Dead Sea Scrolls*. 237, 272, 265, 332.
[109] Shanks, Hershel. *Mystery and Meaning*. 172-176.
[110] Ibid., 76.
[111] Charlesworth, James H. *Bible and the Dead Sea Scrolls*. 133, 301, 318.
[112] Schiffman, Lawrence H. *Reclaiming the Dead Sea Scrolls*. xvii.
[113] Ibid., 73-76.
[114] Ibid.

[115] Shanks, Hershel. *Mystery and Meaning.* 64-74, 82, 158-160.
[116] "Dead Sea Scrolls 75th Anniversary." *Bible Study Magazine,* 2022, 30-43.
[117] VanderKam, James C., and Peter Flint. *Meaning of the Dead Sea Scrolls.* 332, 344.
[118] DeSalvo, John. *History and Myths Revealed.* 155-159, 172.
[119] Shanks, Hershel. *Understanding the Dead Sea Scrolls.* 193-196, 201.
[120] Yadin, Yigael. *Message of the Scrolls.* 14.
[121] "Aleppo Codex." Wikipedia. September 19, 2021. https://en.wikipedia.org/wiki/Aleppo_Codex.
[122] "Biblical Literature: Apocrypha and Pseudepigrapha | Encyclopedia.com"-. https://www.encyclopedia.com/environment/encyclopedias-almanacs-transcripts-and-maps/biblical-literature-apocrypha-and-pseudepigrapha.
[123] "Bar Kokhba Revolt | History & Facts | Britannica." Britannica. https://www.britannica.com/event/Bar-Kokhba-Revolt.
[124] McClure, Bruce. "What Is the Common Era? | Human World | EarthSky." Earthsky. November 6, 2020. https://earthsky.org/human-world/definition-common-era-bce-ce-bc-ad/.
[125] "Apocrypha." Oxford Reference. https://www.oxfordreference.com/display/10.1093/oi/authority.20110803095546561.
[126] "Circumcision, a Symbol of the Jews' Covenant with God." Haaretz. https://www.haaretz.com/jewish/2015-08-26/ty-articlecircumcision-a-symbol-of-the-jews-covenant-with-god/0000017f-e37d-d9aa-afff-fb7d02fb0000.
[127] "BBC - Religions - Christianity: Circumcision." BBC. https://www.bbc.co.uk/religion/religions/christianity/christianethics/circumcision.shtml#:~:text=Christianity%20a 20circumcision.
[128] "Codex." Wikipedia. October 25, 2019. https://en.wikipedia.org/wiki/Codex.
[129] "Deuterocanonical Books." Wikipedia. November 11, 2019. https://en.wikipedia.org/wiki/Deuterocanonical_books.

[130] King, Justin. "Dead Sea Scrolls." World History Encyclopedia. https://www.worldhistory.org/Dead_Sea_Scrolls/.
[131] "Christian Eschatology." Wikipedia. September 16, 2019. https://en.wikipedia.org/wiki/Christian_eschatology.
[132] "Extracanonical." Merriam-Webster. https://www.merriam-webster.com/dictionary/extracanonical.
[133] "Florilegium." Wikipedia. February 24, 2024. https://en.wikipedia.org/wiki/Florilegium.
[134] Davies, Philip "Dead Sea Scrolls." *Britannica.* https://www.britannica.com/topic/Dead-Sea-Scrolls.
[135] "Halakha." Wikipedia. May 11, 2019. https://en.wikipedia.org/wiki/Halakha.
[136] "Hasmonean Dynasty." 2023. Wikipedia. July 30, 2023. https://en.wikipedia.org/wiki/Hasmonean_dynasty.
[137] "Achievements and Decline of the Hellenistic Age | Britannica." Britannica. https://www.britannica.com/summary/Hellenistic-Age.
[138] "Hellenistic Greece." HISTORY. February 4, 2010. https://www.history.com/topics/ancient-greece/hellenistic-greece.
[139] "Intertestamental Period." Wikipedia. October 26, 2022. https://en.wikipedia.org/wiki/Intertestamental_period.
[140] "Khirbet Edh-Dharih." 2024. Wikipedia. April 5, 2024. https://en.wikipedia.org/wiki/Khirbet_edh-Dharih.
[141] "Masoretes | Hebrew School." Britannica. https://www.britannica.com/topic/Masoretes.
[142] "Masoretic Text | Jewish Bible | Britannica." *Britannica.* https://www.britannica.com/topic/Masoretic-text.
[143] "Melchizedek." Wikipedia. March 14, 2023. https://en.wikipedia.org/wiki/Melchizedek.
[144] "Mishna | Jewish Laws." Britannica. https://www.britannica.com/topic/Mishna.
[145] "Paleo." *Collins English Dictionary - Complete & Unabridged 2012 Digital-Edition.* https://www.collinsdictionary.com/dictionary/english/paleo
[146] "Explore the Pentateuch: The First 5 Books of the Bible." Learn Religions. https://www.learnreligions.com/what-is-the-pentateuch-700745.

[147] "Pesher." Jewish Virtual Library.
https://www.jewishvirtuallibrary.org/pesher#google_vignette.
[148] "Procurator | Encyclopedia.com." Encyclopedia.
https://www.encyclopedia.com/philosophy-and-religion/bible/bible-general/procurator.
[149] "Pseudepigrapha - What We Believe Scripture Text." Montevista Church of Christ.
https://montevistacoc.com/download-file/2022/03/Pseudepigrapha-What-We-Believe-Scripture-Text.pdf
[150] "Rabbi | Judaism." *Britannica*.
https://www.britannica.com/topic/rabbi.
[151] "Samaritan Pentateuch." Wikipedia. March 28, 2024.
https://en.wikipedia.org/wiki/Samaritan_Pentateuch.
[152] "Sect." Wikipedia. December 26, 2020.
https://en.wikipedia.org/wiki/Sect.
[153] "Sectarian." Merriam-Webster.
https://www.merriam-webster.com/dictionary/sectarian.
[154] "Septuagint." Wikipedia. December 6, 2019.
https://en.wikipedia.org/wiki/Septuagint.
[155] "Tetragrammaton." Wikipedia. October 23, 2020.
https://en.wikipedia.org/wiki/Tetragrammaton.
[156] "Talmud." Jewish Encyclopedia.
https://www.jewishencyclopedia.com/articles/14213-talmud.
[157] "Hebrew Bible." Wikipedia.
https://en.wikipedia.org/wiki/Hebrew_Bible#:~:text=Tanakh%20is%20an%20acronym%2C%20made.
[158] "Targum." Wikipedia. February 8, 2024.
https://en.wikipedia.org/wiki/Targum.
[159] "Torah." Wikipedia. May 31, 2019.
https://en.wikipedia.org/wiki/Torah.
[160] "Definition of WADI." Merriam-Webster. 2019.
https://www.merriam-webster.com/dictionary/wadi.
[161] "Yaḥad | Encyclopedia.com." Encyclopedia.
https://www.encyclopedia.com/religion/encyclopedias-almanacs-transcripts-and-maps/yahad.
[162] Cronin, Richard J. 1956. "Edmund Wilson and the Dead Sea Scrolls." *Philippine Studies* 4 (3): 411–31.
https://www.jstor.org/stable/42720344.

[163] Avigad, N. 1967. "E. L. Sukenik — the Man and His Work." *Eretz-Israel: Archaeological, Historical and Geographical Studies:* IX–XI.
https://www.jstor.org/stable/23616858.
[164] "Emanuel Tov." Wikipedia. March 6, 2024.
https://en.wikipedia.org/wiki/Emanuel_Tov.
[165] Yardley, William. 2012. "Frank Moore Cross, Biblical Scholar, Dies at 91." *The New York Times*, October 20, 2012, sec. U.S.
https://www.nytimes.com/2012/10/20/us/frank-moore-cross-biblical-scholar-and-dead-sea-scrolls-interpreter-diesat-91.html.
[166] "Géza Vermes." Wikipedia. January 23, 2024.
https://en.wikipedia.org/wiki/G%C3%A9za_Vermes.
[167] "Died: Editor Who Saved Biblical Archaeology from Academics." News & Reporting. February 8, 2021.
https://www.christianitytoday.com/news/2021/february/died-hershel-shanks-biblical-archaeology-review-dead-sea-sc.html.
[168] "Józef Milik." Wikipedia. August 22, 2023.
https://en.wikipedia.org/wiki/J%C3%B3zef_Milik.
[169] "James C. VanderKam // Institute for Advanced Study // University of Notre Dame." Institute for Advanced Study.
https://ndias.nd.edu/fellows/vanderkam-james-c/.
[170] "John M. Allegro." Wikipedia. November 16, 2019.
https://en.wikipedia.org/wiki/John_M._Allegro.
[171] "John Strugnell." Wikipedia. January 13, 2024.
https://en.wikipedia.org/wiki/John_Strugnell.
[172] "John C. Trever, 90; His Photos of Dead Sea Scrolls Preserved the Documents for Biblical Research." Los Angeles Times. May 4, 2006.
https://www.latimes.com/archives/la-xpm-2006-may-04-me-trever4-story.html.
[173] "Unfurling the Claims to the Dead Sea Scrolls." The Globe and Mail. April-18,-2009.
https://www.theglobeandmail.com/news/world/unfurling-the-claims-to-the-dead-sea-scrolls/article4273124/.
[174] "Lawrence Schiffman." Wikipedia. September 22, 2019.
https://en.wikipedia.org/wiki/Lawrence_Schiffman.

[175] "Martin G. Abegg on Electronic Dead Sea Scrolls." Brian W. Davidson.-September-20,-2013. https://brianwdavidson.com/2013/09/20/interview-with-martin-g-abegg-on-electronic-dead-sea-scrolls/.
[176] Athanasius Yeshue Samuel." Wikipedia. January 6, 2023. https://en.wikipedia.org/wiki/Athanasius_Yeshue_Samuel.
[177] "Michael O. Wise. "University of Northwestern, St. Paul. https://www.unwsp.edu/bio/michael-o-wise/.
[178] "Dead Sea Scrolls." Wikipedia. March 18, 2019. https://en.wikipedia.org/wiki/Dead_Sea_scrolls.
[179] Norman Golb | near Eastern Languages and Civilizations." Nelc.uchicago.edu. https://nelc.uchicago.edu/people/norman-golb.
[180] "Robert Eisenman." Wikipedia. November 5, 2019. https://en.wikipedia.org/wiki/Robert_Eisenman.
[181] "Roland de Vaux." Wikipedia. February 15, 2024. https://en.wikipedia.org/wiki/Roland_de_Vaux.
[182] "Yigael Yadin | Israeli General and Archaeologist | Britannica." Britannica.com. https://www.britannica.com/biography/Yigael-Yadin

# Appendix D
## Bibliography

### Books

Abegg, Martin Jr., Peter Flint, and Eugene Ulrich. *The Dead Sea Scrolls: The Oldest Known Bible Translated for the First Time into English.* New York: HarperCollins, 1990.

Allegro, John. *The Mystery of the Dead Sea Scrolls Revealed.* New York: Gramercy Publishing Company, 1981.

Arnold, Bill T. and Bryan E. Beyer. *Encountering the Old Testament: A Christian Survey (Encountering Biblical Studies).* Grand Rapids: Baker Publishing Group, 2008.

Barker, Kenneth L, General Editor. *The NIV Study Bible.* Grand Rapids: Zondervan, 2011.

Biondi, Lee. *From the Dead Sea Scrolls to the Bible in America.* Camarillo: Squire Resources, Inc., 2009.

Burrows, Millar. *The Dead Sea Scrolls.* New York: The Viking Press, 1955.

Campbell, Jonathan G. *Dead Sea Scrolls: The Complete Story.* Berkeley: Ulysses Press, 1998.

Carson, D.A. General Editor. *NIV Biblical Theology Study Bible.* Grand Rapids: Zondervan, 2018.

Charlesworth, James H. *The Bible and the Dead Sea Scrolls: Volume One: Scripture and the Scrolls.* Waco: Baylor Unversity Press, 2006.

Collins, John J. *The Dead Sea Scrolls: A Biography*. Princeton: Princeton University Press, 2013.

Cross, Frank Moore. *The Dead Sea Scrolls*. Washington D.C.: Biblical Archeological Society and Society of Biblical Literature, 2007.

Cross, Frank Moore. *The Ancient Library of Qumran, 3$^{rd}$ Edition*. Minneapolis: Fortress Press, 1995.

Davies, Philip R. *Cities of the Biblical World: Qumran*. Guildford: Lutterworth Press, 1982.

Davies, Philip R., George J. Brooke, and Phillip R. Callaway. *The Complete World of the Dead Sea Scrolls*. New York: Thames & Hudson Ltd., 2002.

DeSalvo, John. *Dead Sea Scrolls: Their History and Myths Revealed*. New York: Fall River Press, 2014.

Eisenman, Robert H. and Michael Wise. *The Dead Sea Scrolls Uncovered*. New York: Barnes & Noble Publishing Inc. 2004.

Herron, Ellen Middlebrook, ed. *The Dead Sea Scrolls*. Grand Rapids: The Public Museum of Grand Rapids and Wm B. Eerdmans Publishing Company, 2003.

Fitzmyer, Joseph A. *The Impact of the Dead Sea Scrolls*. Mahwah: Paulist Press, 2009.

General Editor. *NIV Archeological Study Bible*. Grand Rapids: Zondervan, 2005.

Golb, Norman. *Who Wrote the Dead Sea Scrolls? The Search for the Secret of Qumran*. New York: Scribner, 1995.

Hanson, Kenneth. *Dead Sea Scrolls: The Untold Story*. Tulsa: Council Oak Books, 1997.

Henze, Matthias. *Biblical Interpretation at Qumran: Studies in the Dead Sea Scrolls and Related Literature*. Grand Rapids: William B. Eerdmans Publishing Co., 2005.

Kohn, Risa Levitt. *Dead Sea Scrolls*. San Diego: San Diego State University Press, 2007.

Lewis, C S. *Mere Christianity*. New York: HarperCollins Publishers, 1952.

Pfieffer, Charles F. *The Dead Sea Scrolls and the Bible*. Grand Rapids: Baker Book House, 1969.

Rendsburg, Gary A. *The Great Courses: The Dead Sea Scrolls Course Guidebook*. Chantilly: The Teaching Company, 2010.

Shanks, Hershel. *The Mystery and Meaning of the Dead Sea Scrolls*. New York: Random House, 1998.

Shanks, Hershel. *Understanding the Dead Sea Scrolls: A Reader from the Biblical Archaeology Review*. New York: Random House, 1992.

Schiffman, Lawrence H. *Reclaiming the Dead Sea Scrolls: Their True Meaning for Judaism and Christianity*. New York: Doubleday Religious Publishing Group, Inc., 1995

Trevor, John C. *The Untold Story of Qumran*. Westwood: Fleming H. Revell Company, 1965.

Ulrich, Eugene. *The Dead Sea Scrolls and the Origins of the Bible*. Grand Rapids: Wm B. Eerdmans Publishing Company, 1999.

VanderKam, James C. *The Dead Sea Scrolls and the Bible*. Grand Rapids: Wm B. Eerdmans Publishing Company, 2012.

VanderKam, James C. *The Dead Sea Scrolls Today*. Grand Rapids: Wm B. Eerdmans Publishing Company, 1994.

VanderKam, James C. and Peter Flint. *The Meaning of The Dead Sea Scrolls: Their Significance for Understanding the Bible, Judaism, Jesus, and Christianity.* New York: HarperCollins Publishers Inc., 2002.

Vermes, Geza. *The Complete Dead Sea Scrolls in English.* New York: The Penguin Press, 1997.

Wilson, Edmund. *The Scrolls from the Dead Sea.* New York: Oxford University Press, 1955.

Wilson, Edmund. *The Dead Sea Scrolls, 1947-1969.* New York: Oxford University Press, 1969.

Wise, Michael, Martin Abegg Jr., and Edward Cook. *The Dead Sea Scrolls: A New Translation.* New York: HarperSanFrancisco, 1996.

Yadin, Yigael. *The Message of the Scrolls.* New York: Simon & Schuster, Inc., 1957.

## Periodicals/Journals

Baker, J.I., and Emily Joshu, eds. "Dead Sea Scrolls: The Race to Solve an Ancient Mystery." Special Issue, *Life Magazine,* 2022.

Isbouts, Jean-Pierre, ed. "Dead Sea Scrolls: 75 Years Since Their Historic Discovery." Special Issue, *National Geographic Magazine,* 2022.

Ward, Mark, and David Bomar, eds. "Dead Sea Scrolls 75th Anniversary." *Bible Study Magazine* 14, no. 2, January/February, 2022.

## Digital Media

Rendsburg, Gary A. "The Great Courses: The Dead Sea Scrolls." Chantilly: The Teaching Company, 2010.

www.ingramcontent.com/pod-product-compliance
Lightning Source LLC
Chambersburg PA
CBHW051433290426
44109CB00016B/1534